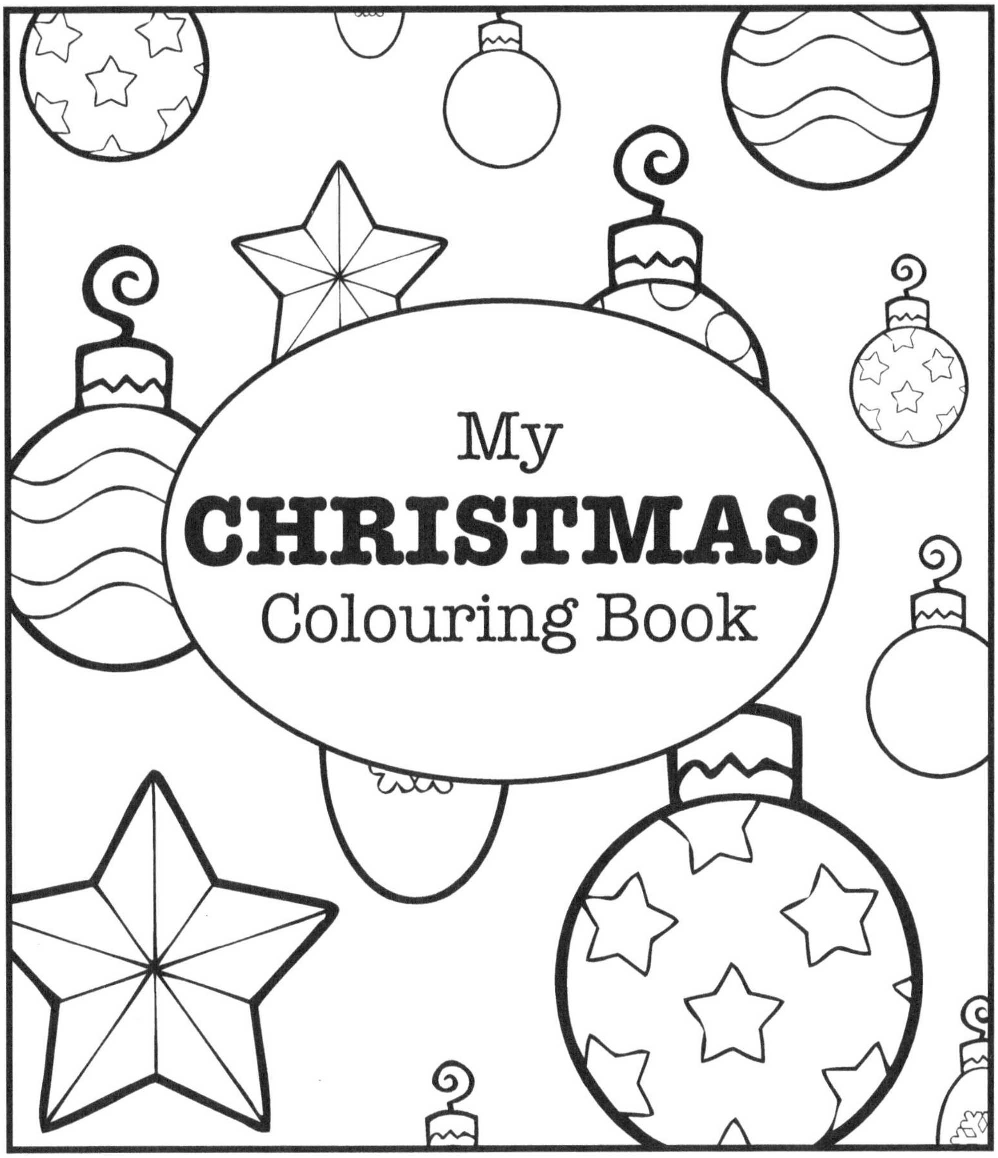

Crazy Colouring for Kids **Book 2**

First published in 2015 by Kyle Craig Publishing

Editor: Alison McNicol

Design: Elizabeth James, Julie Anson, Alison McNicol, Shutterstock, Inc.

ISBN: 978-1-78595-076-6

A CIP record for this book is available from the British Library.

A Kyle Craig Publication

www.kyle-craig.com

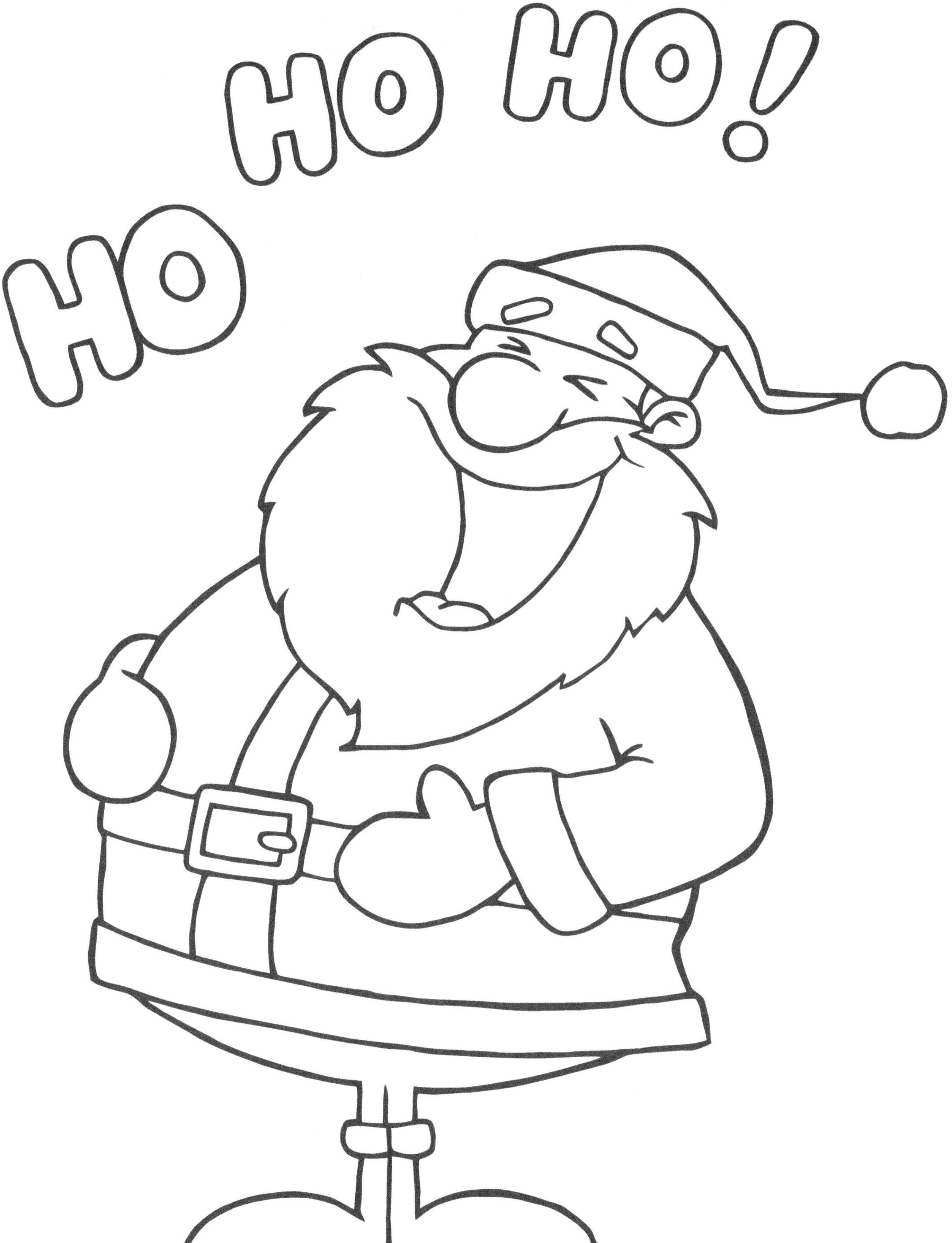
HO HO HO!

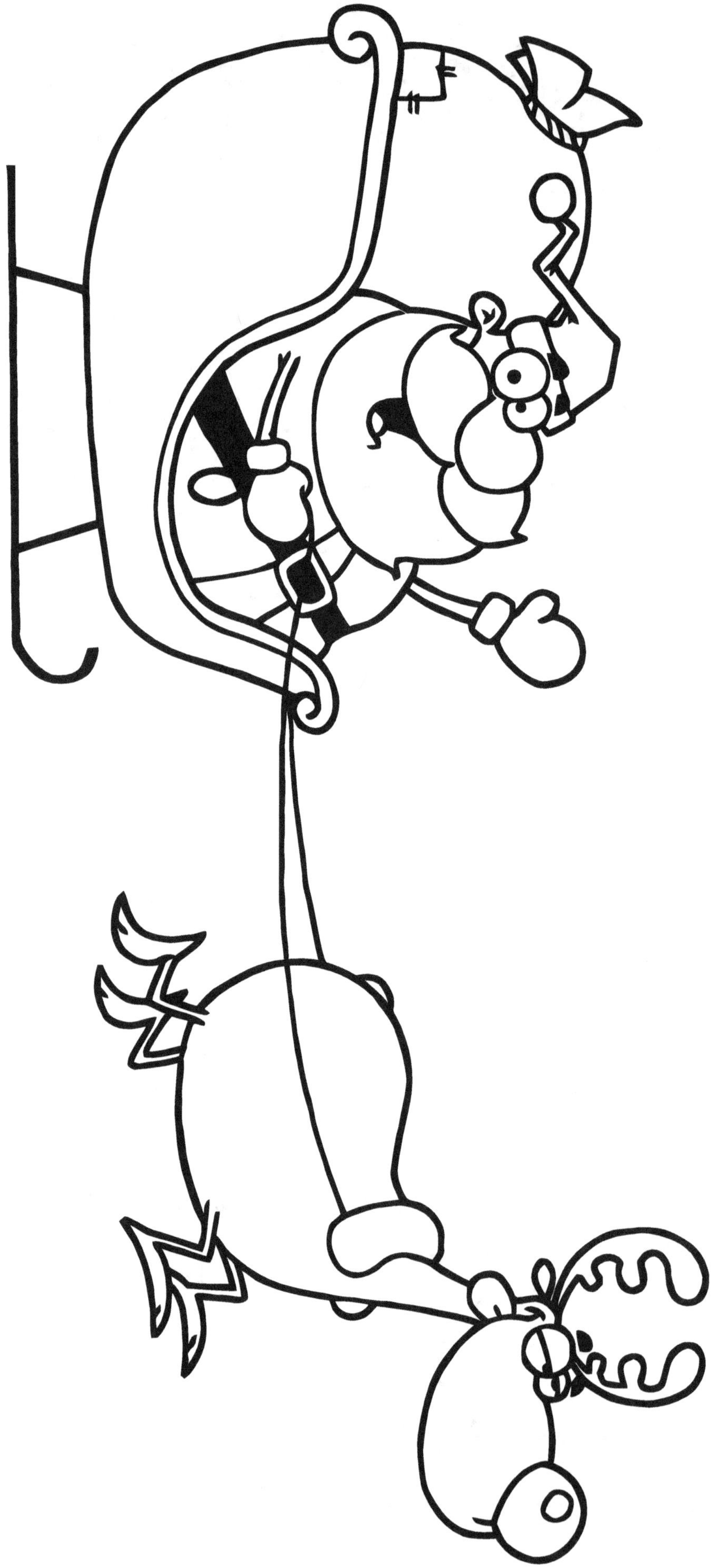

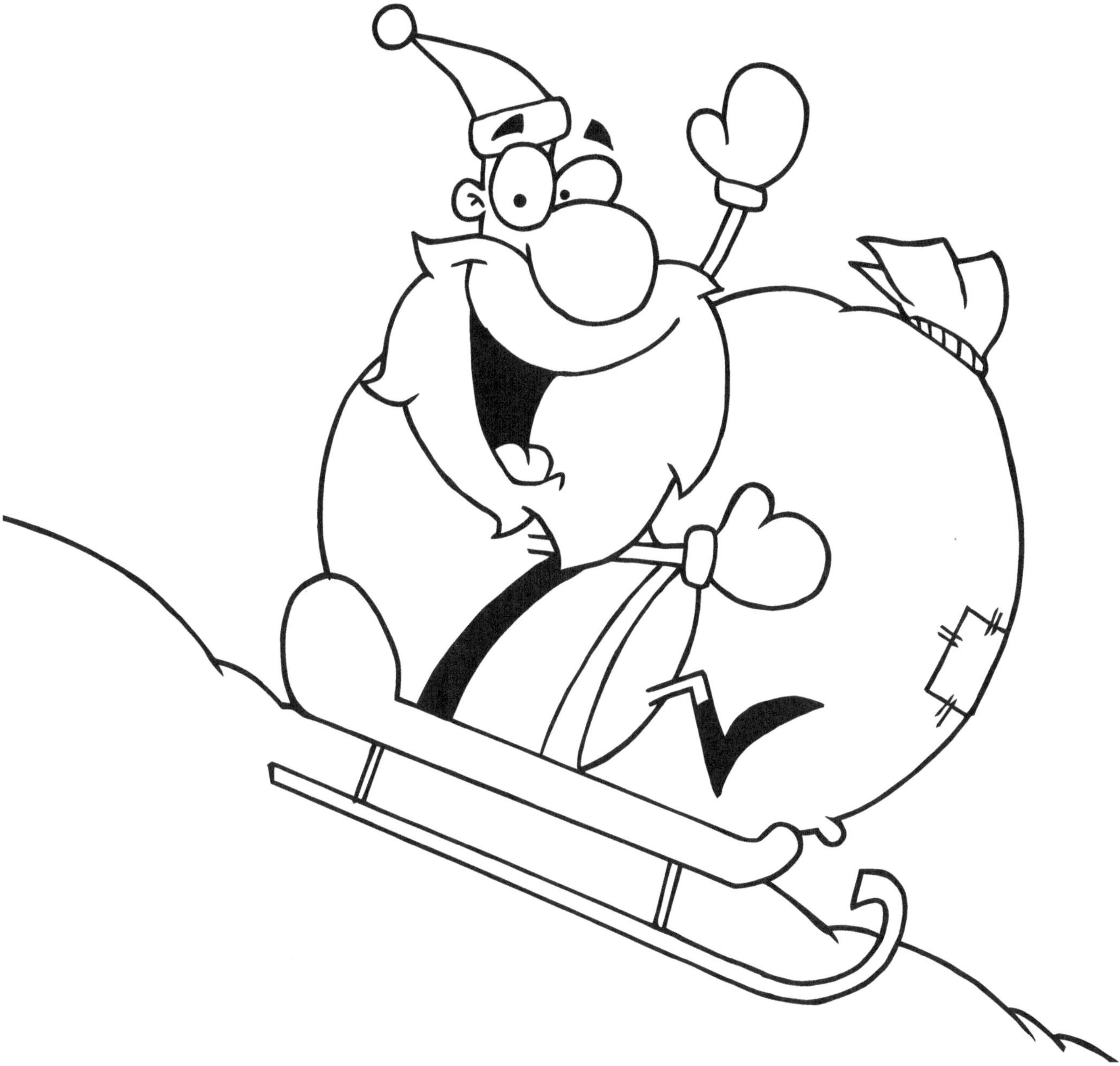

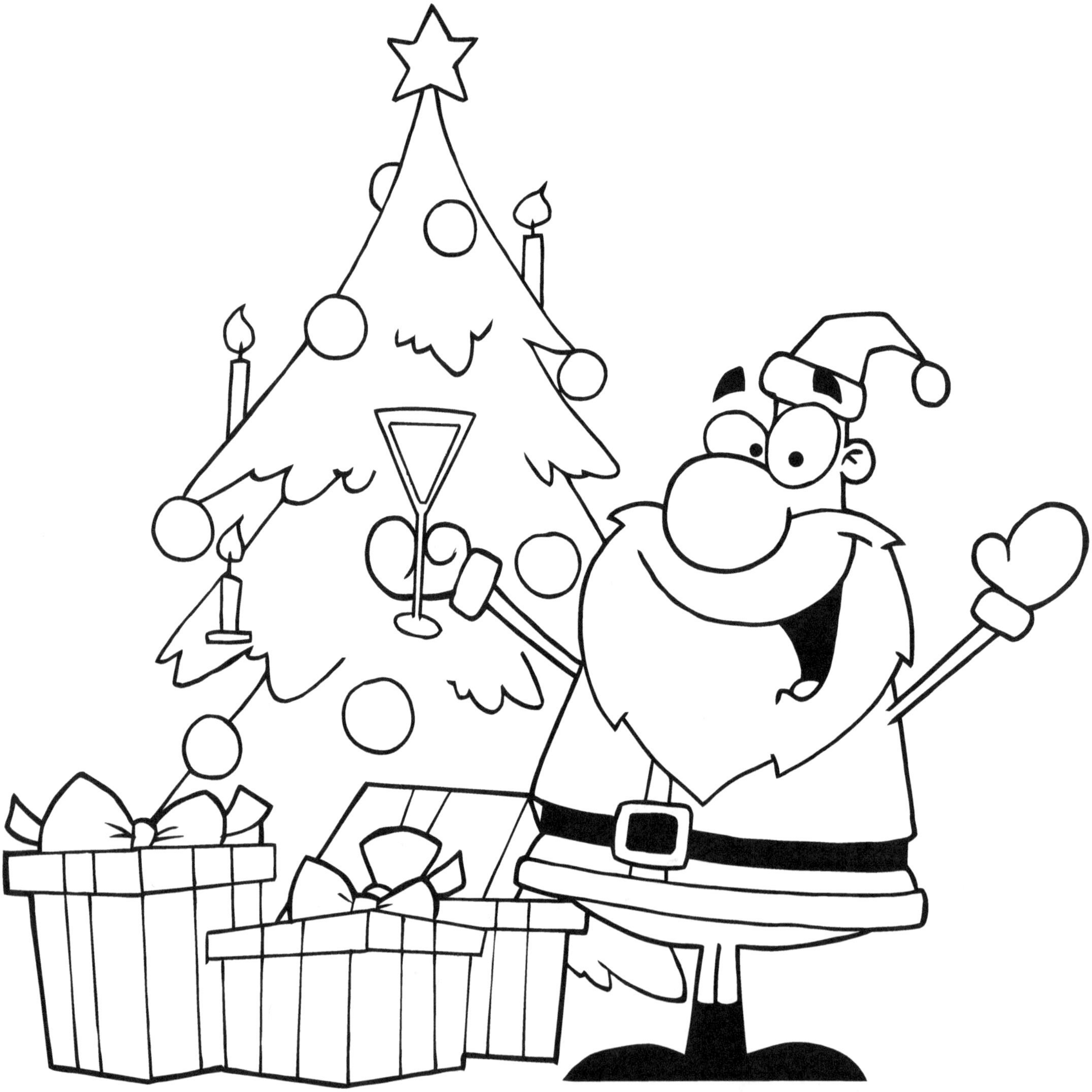

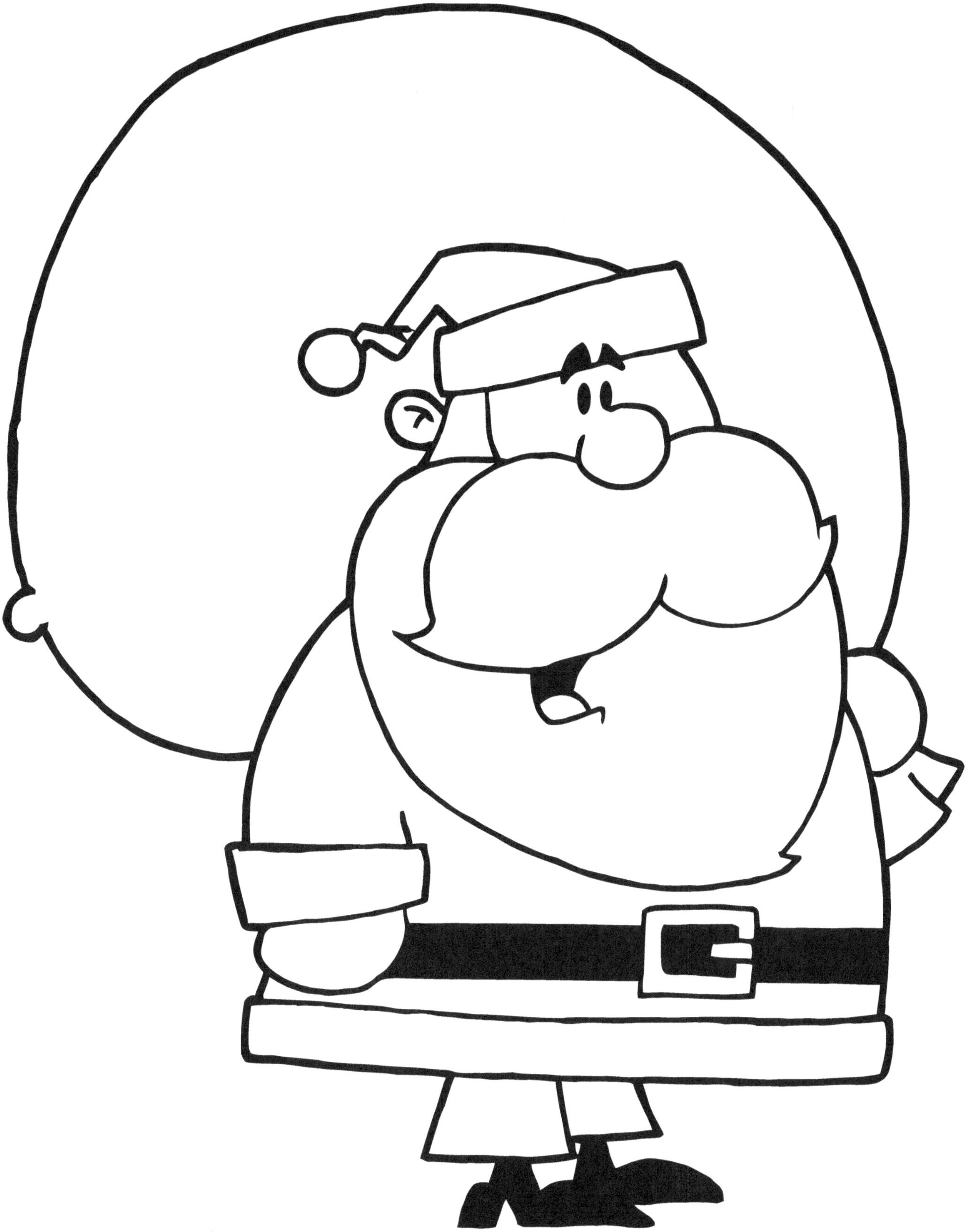

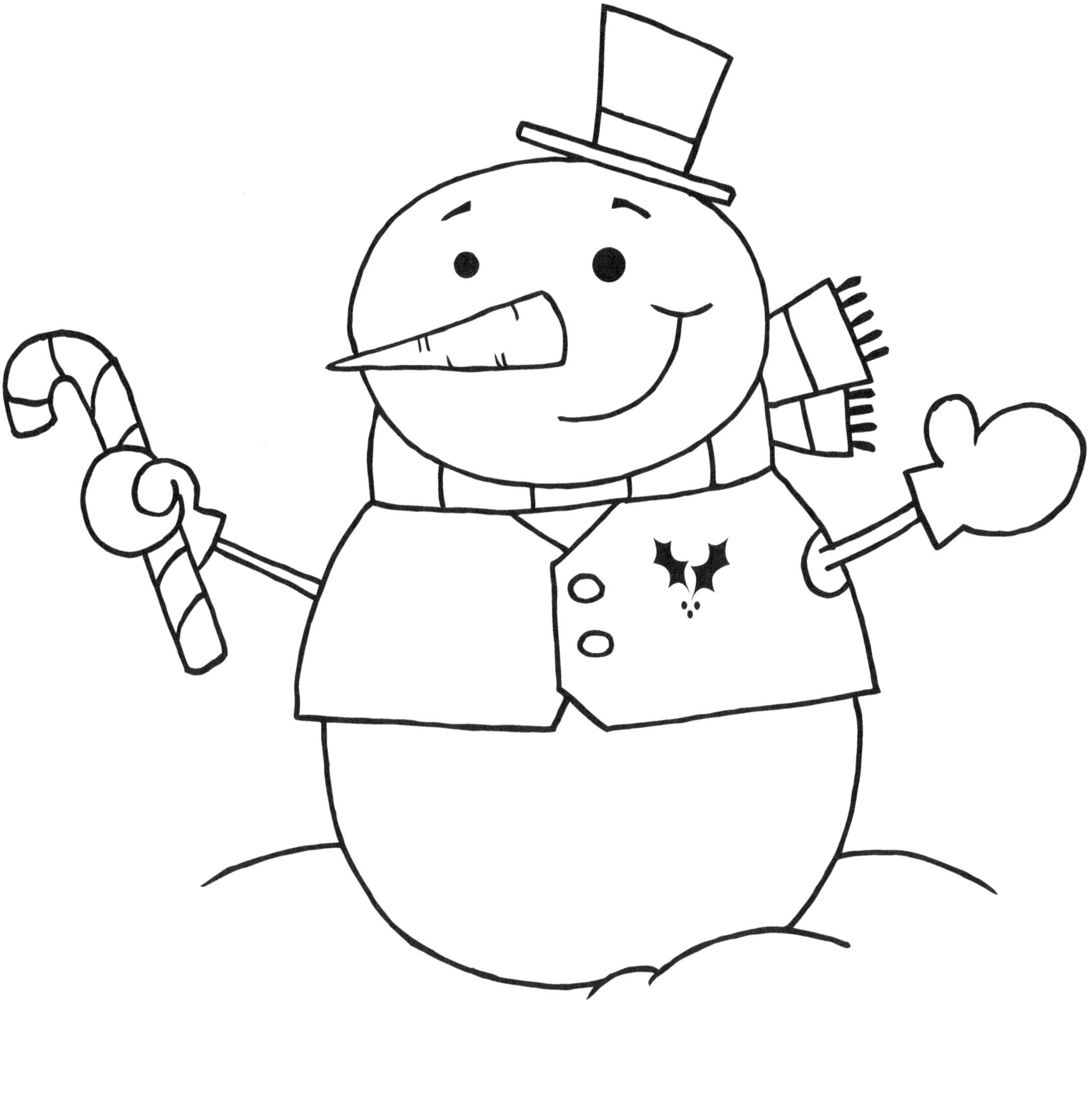

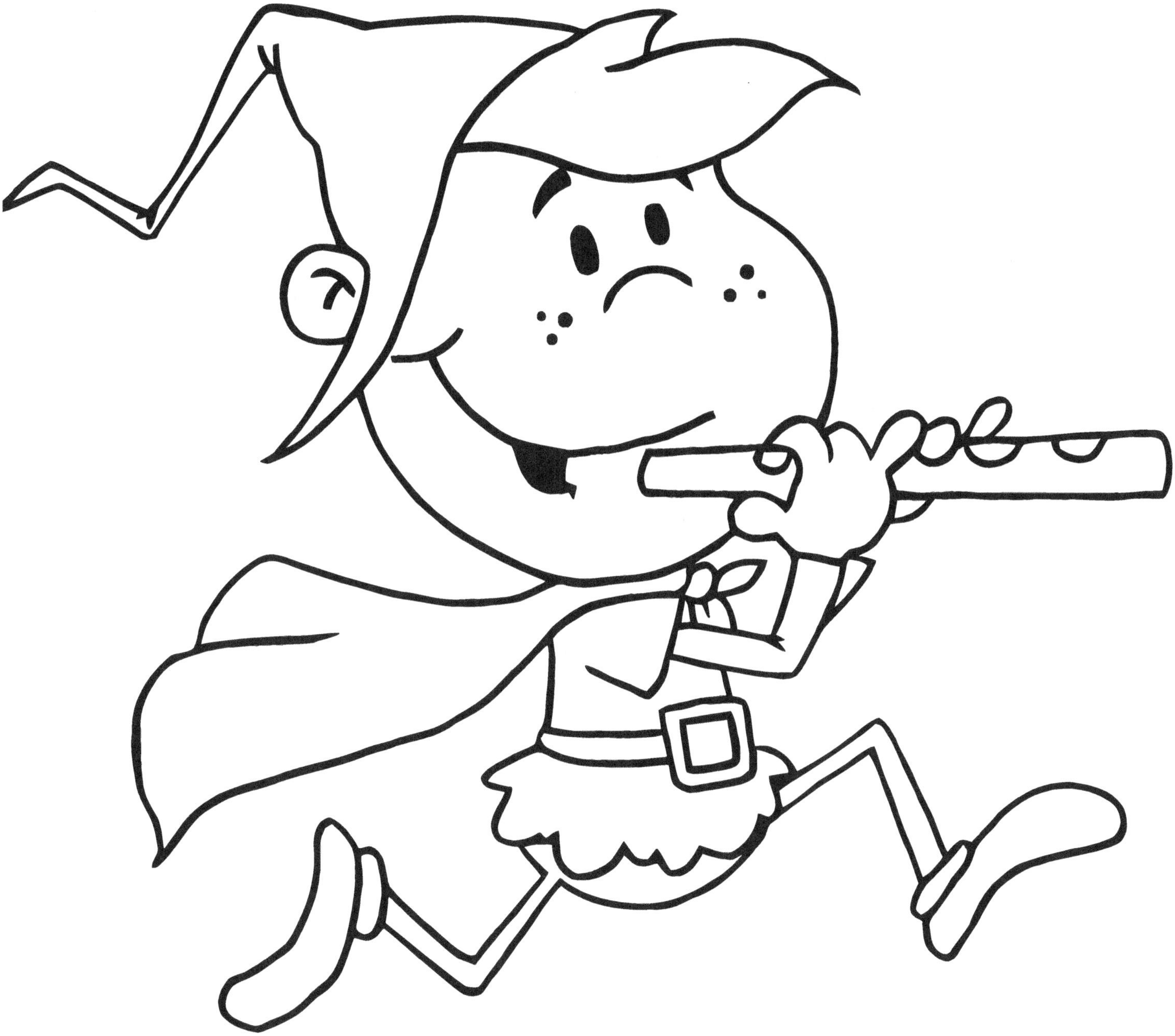

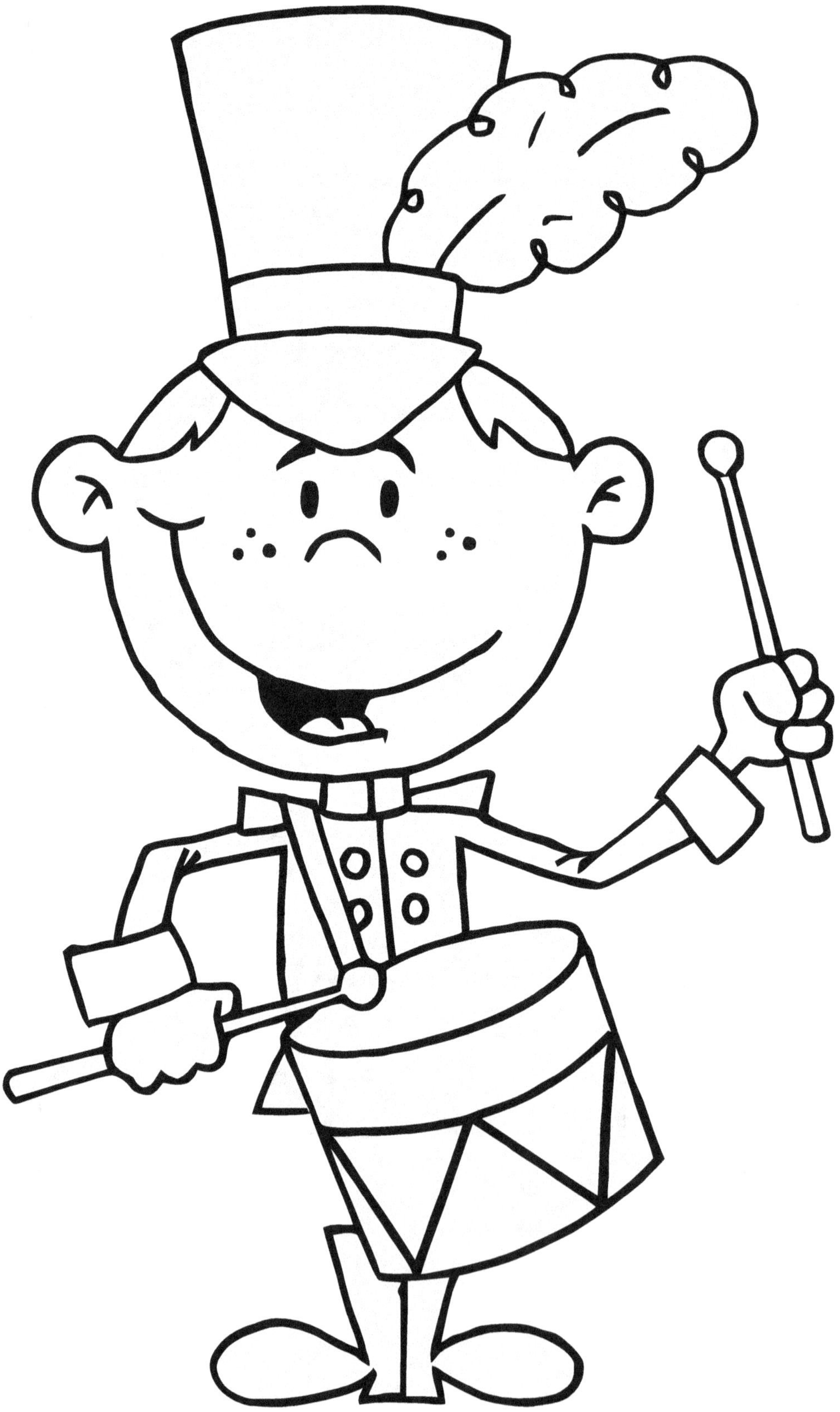

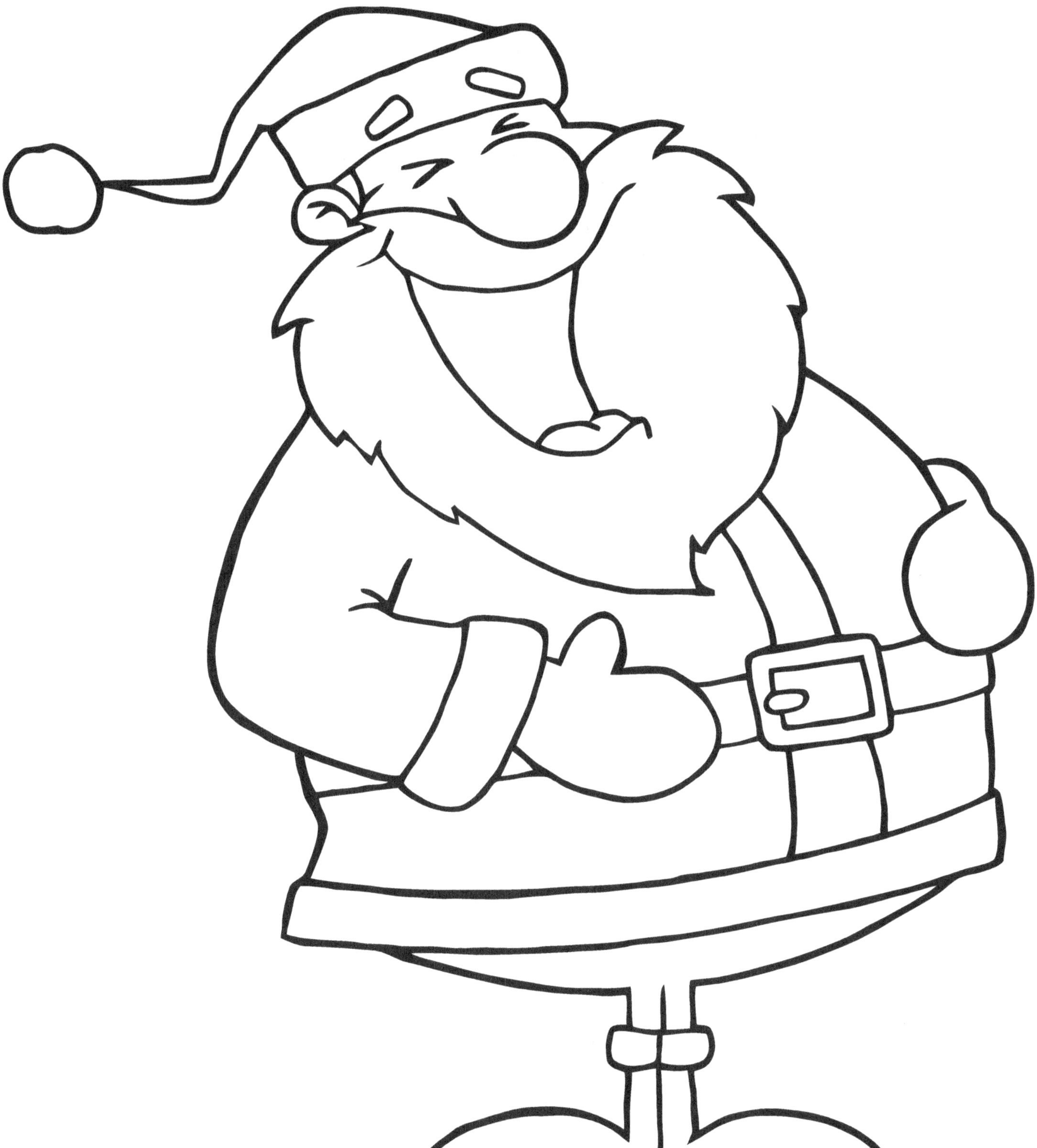

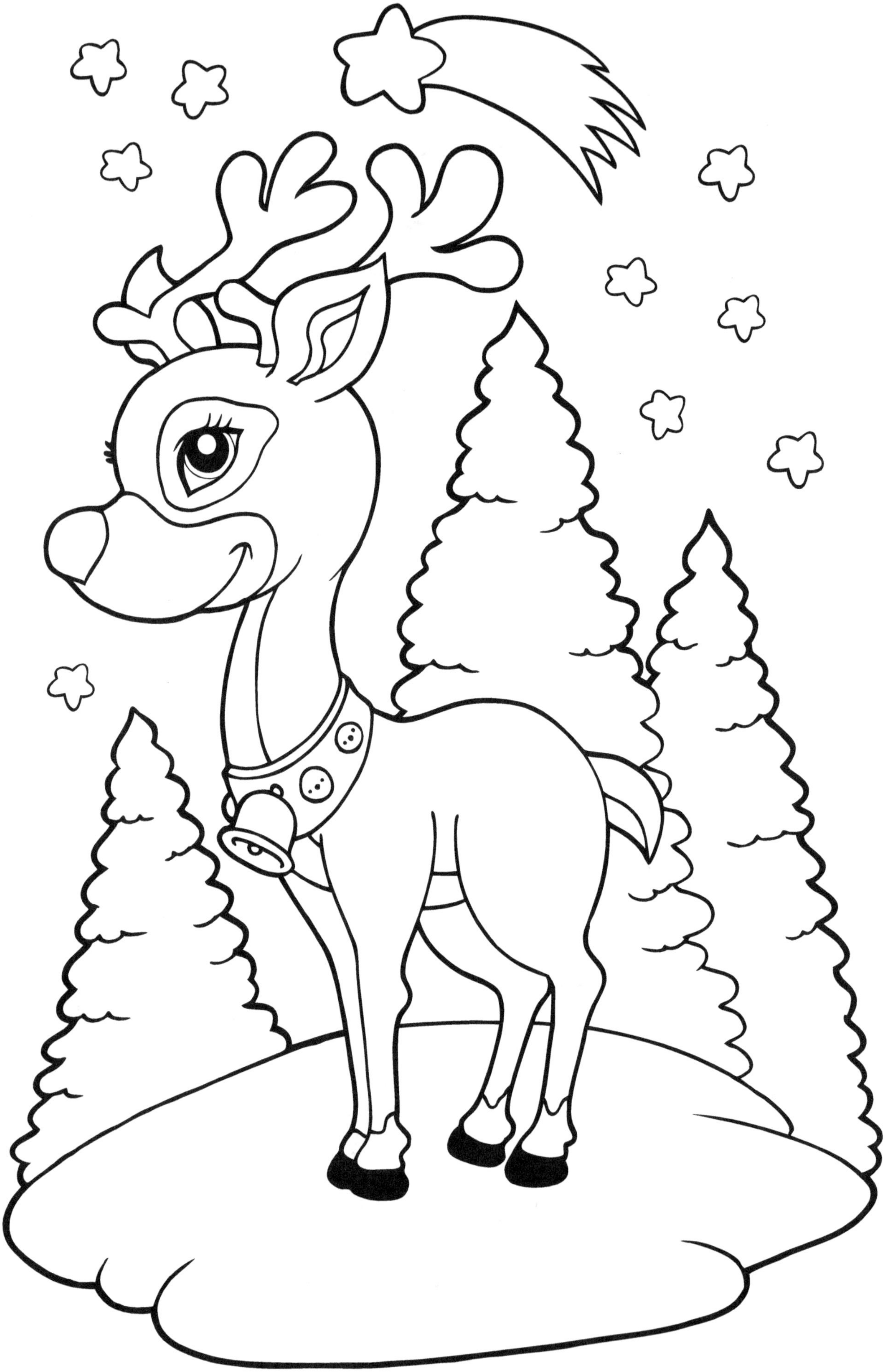

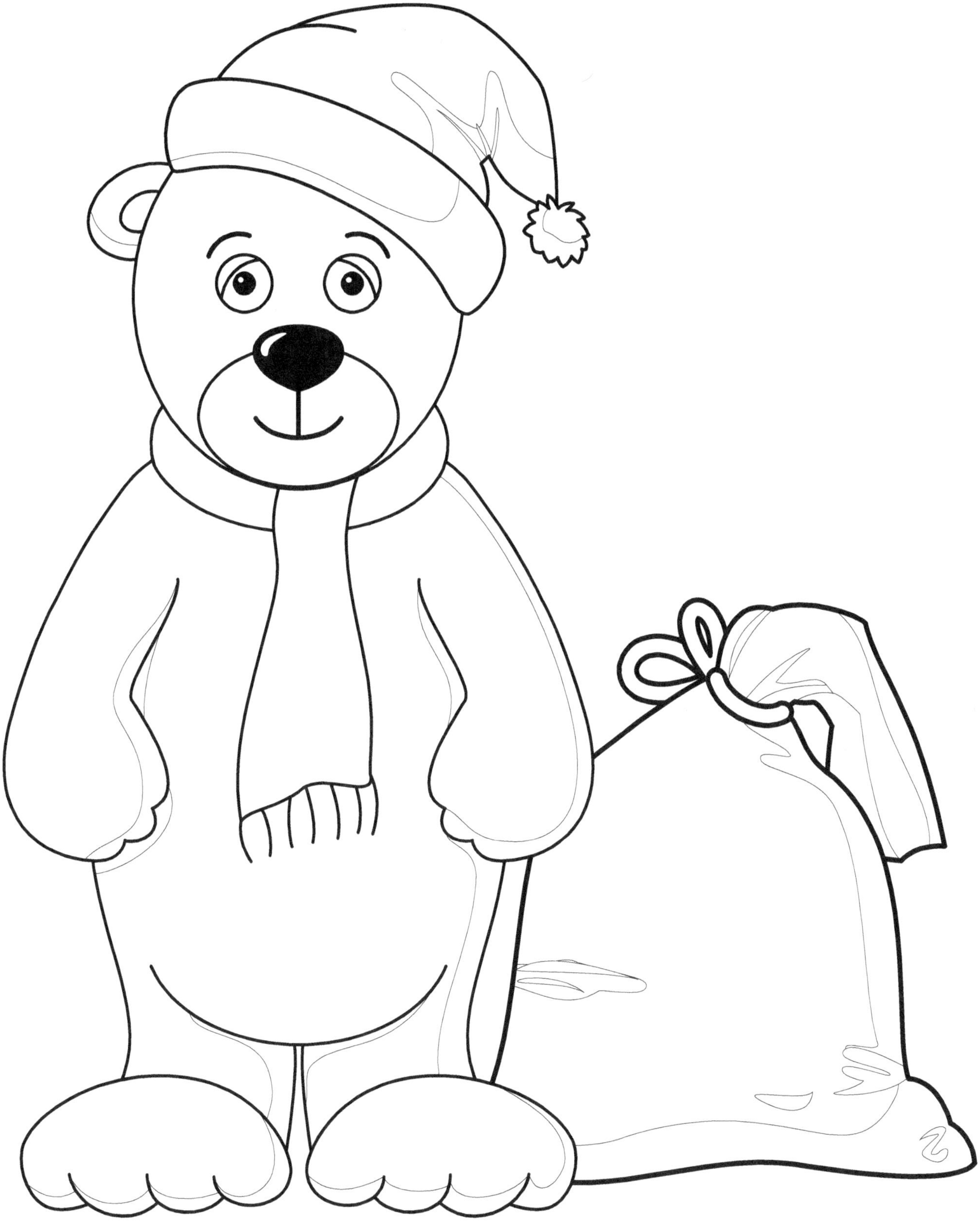

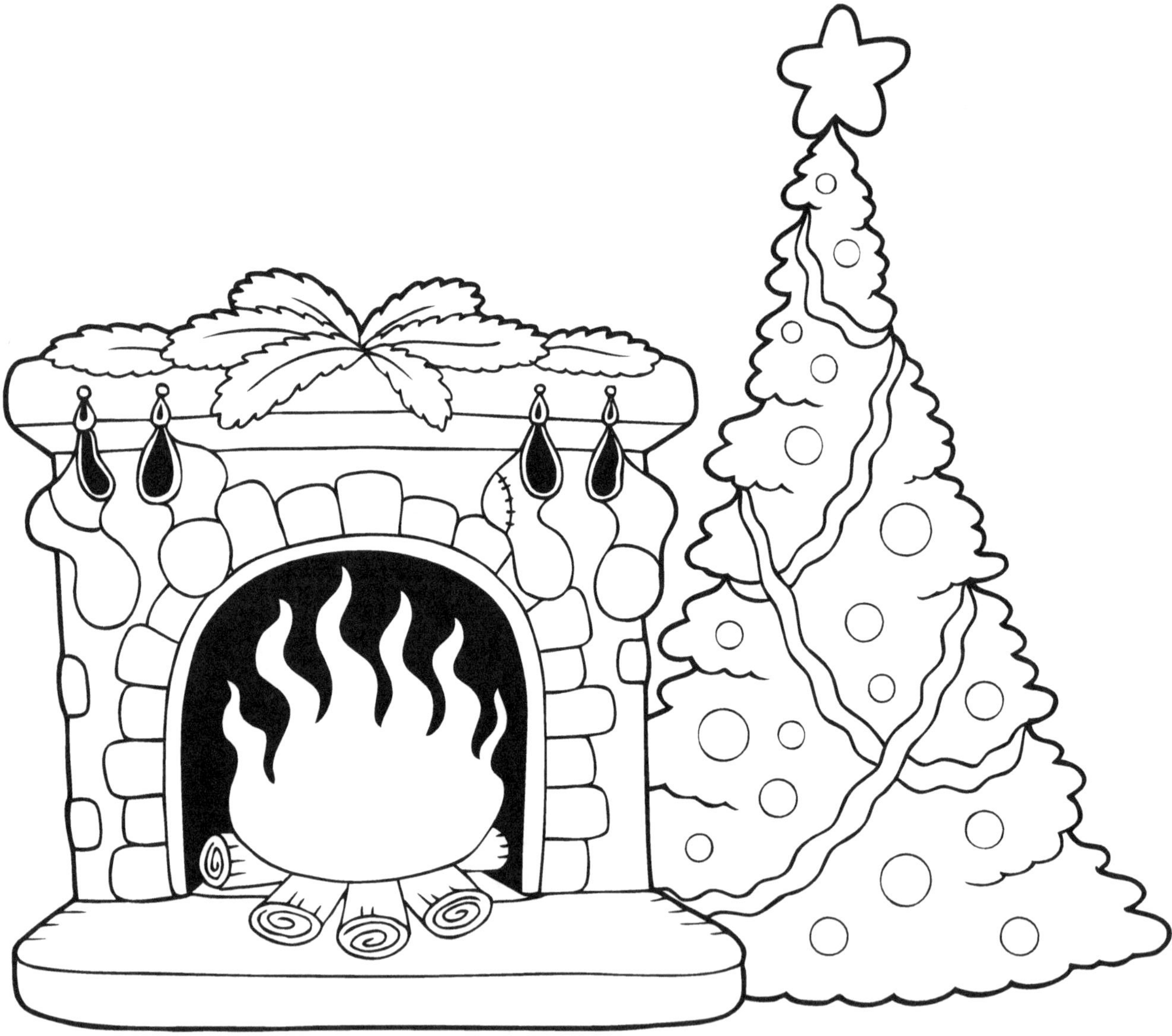

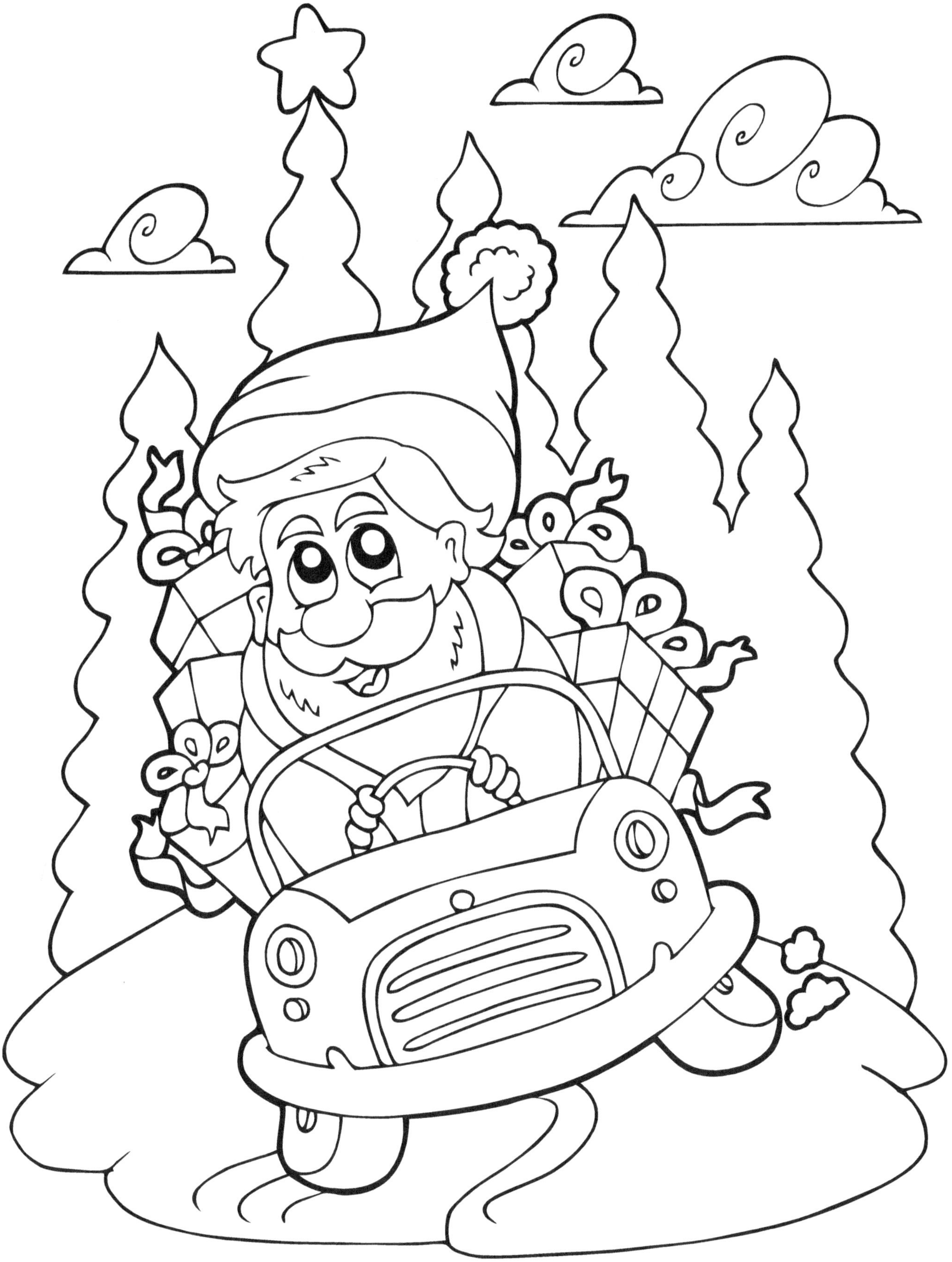

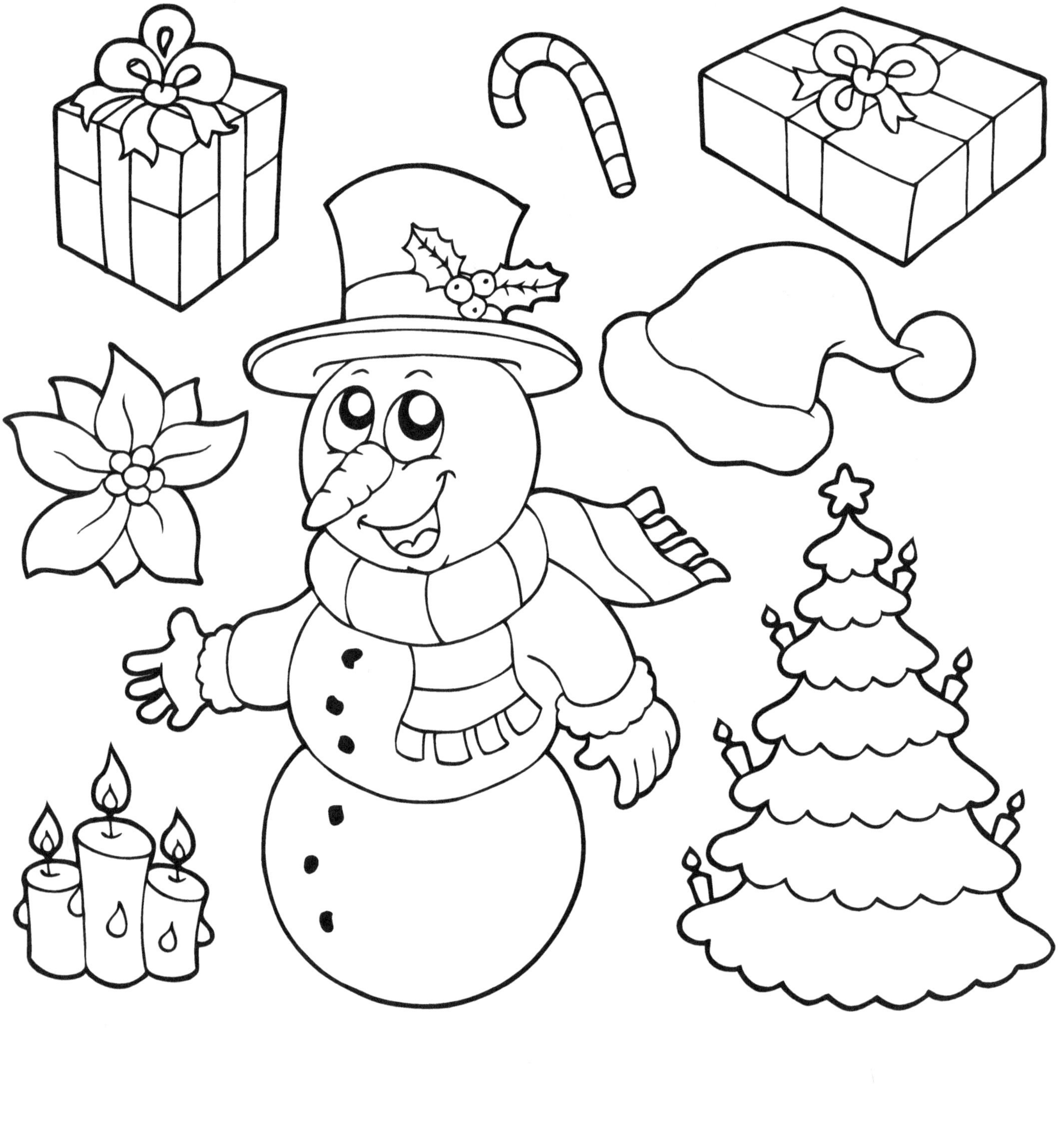

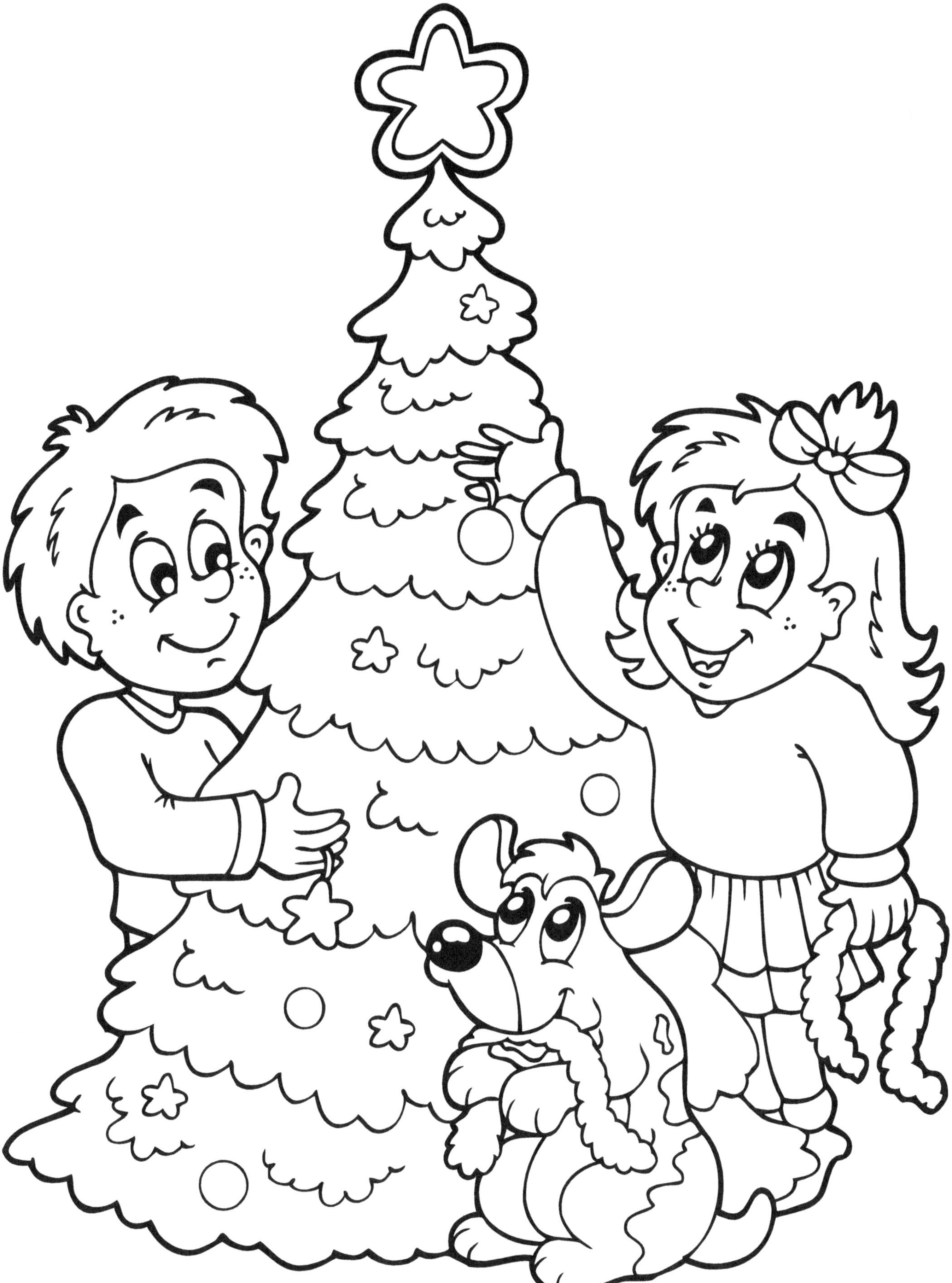

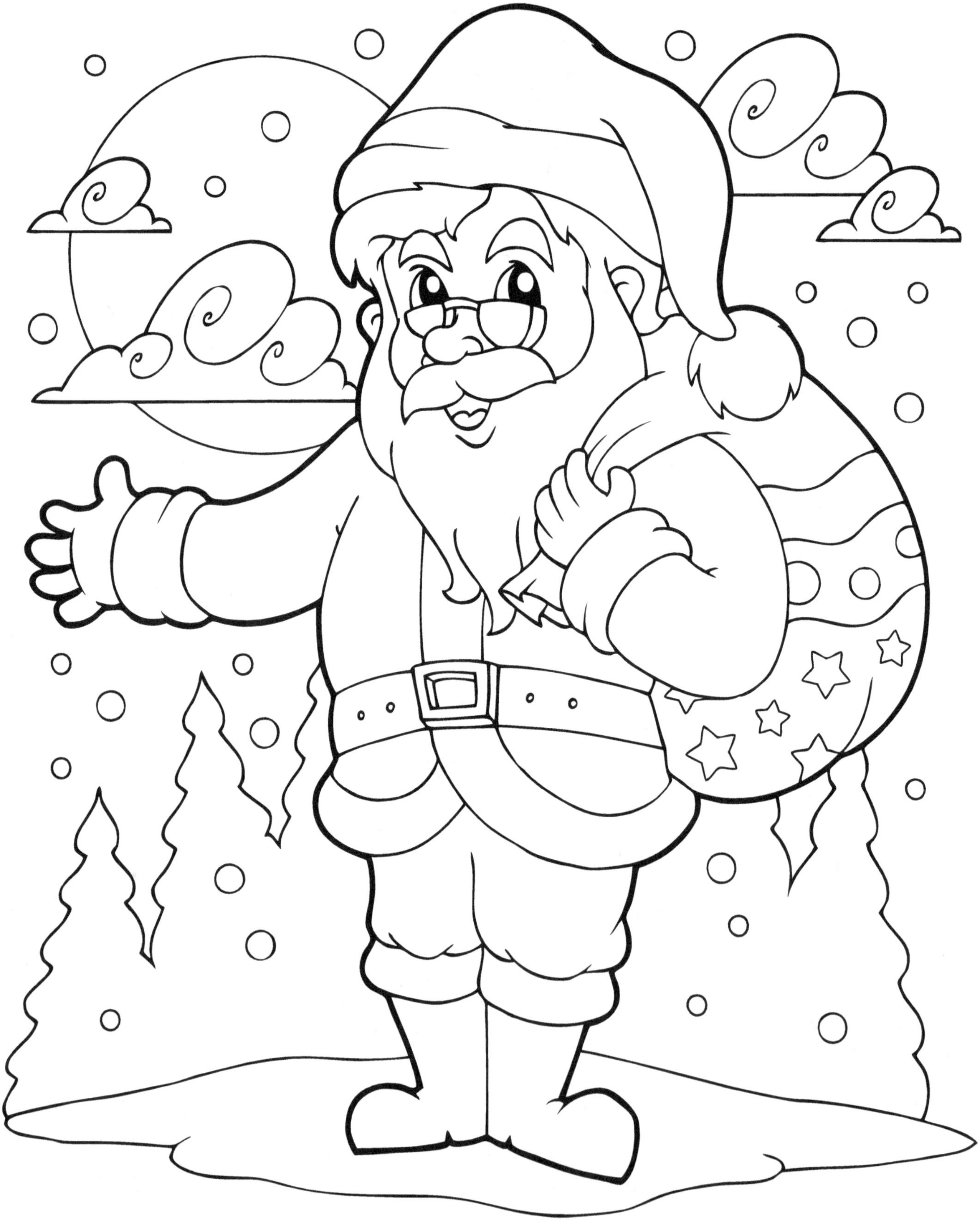

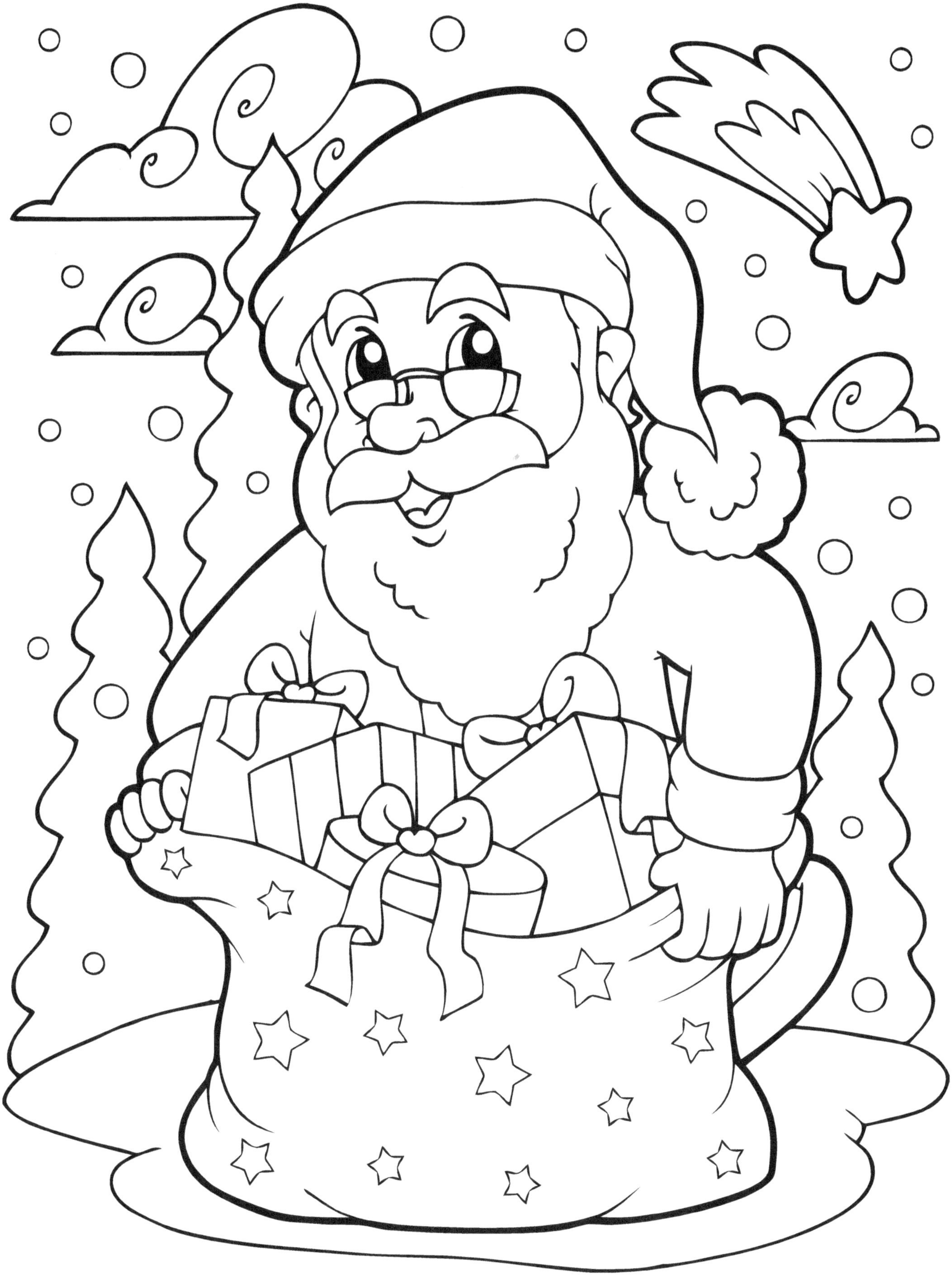

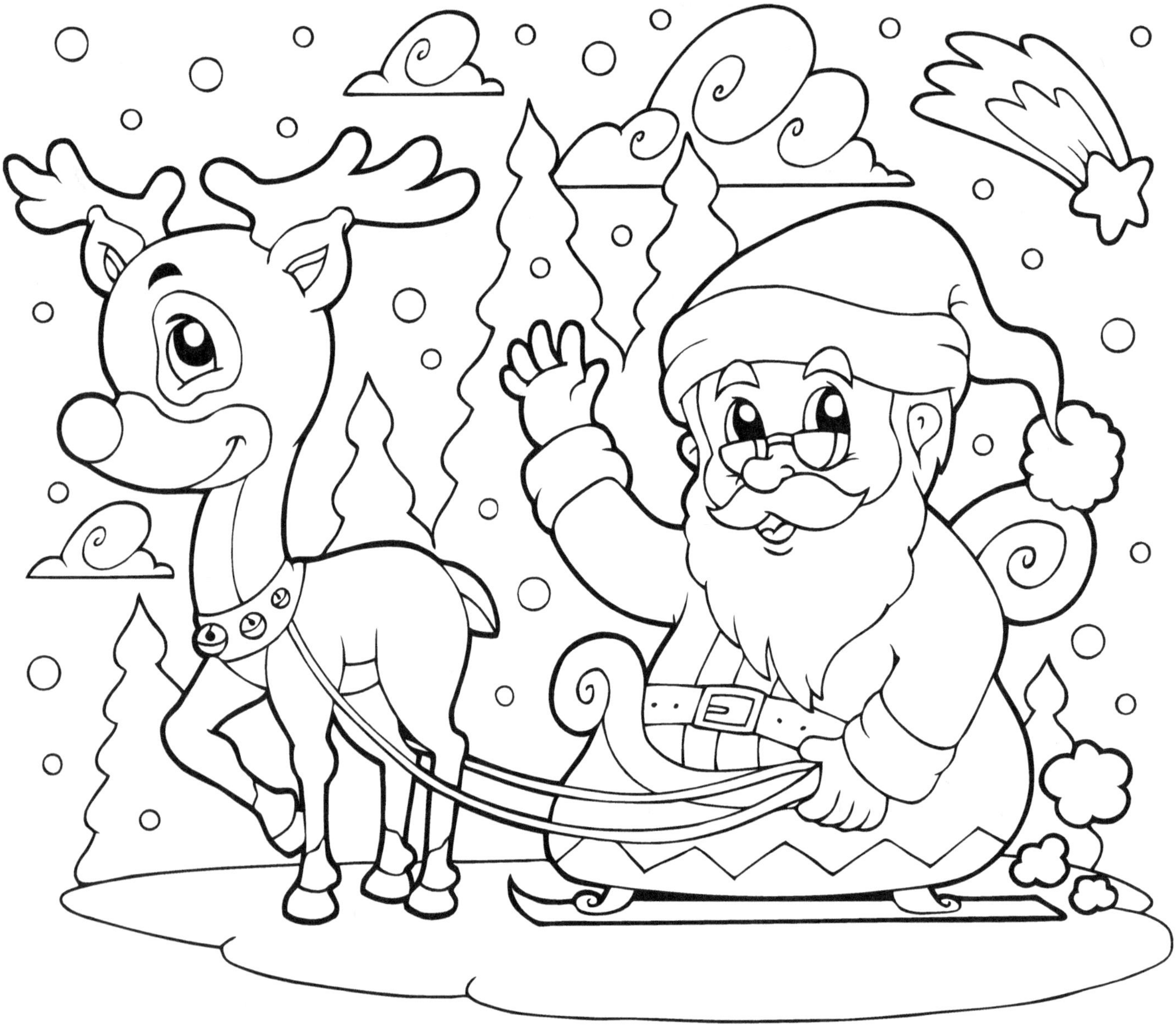

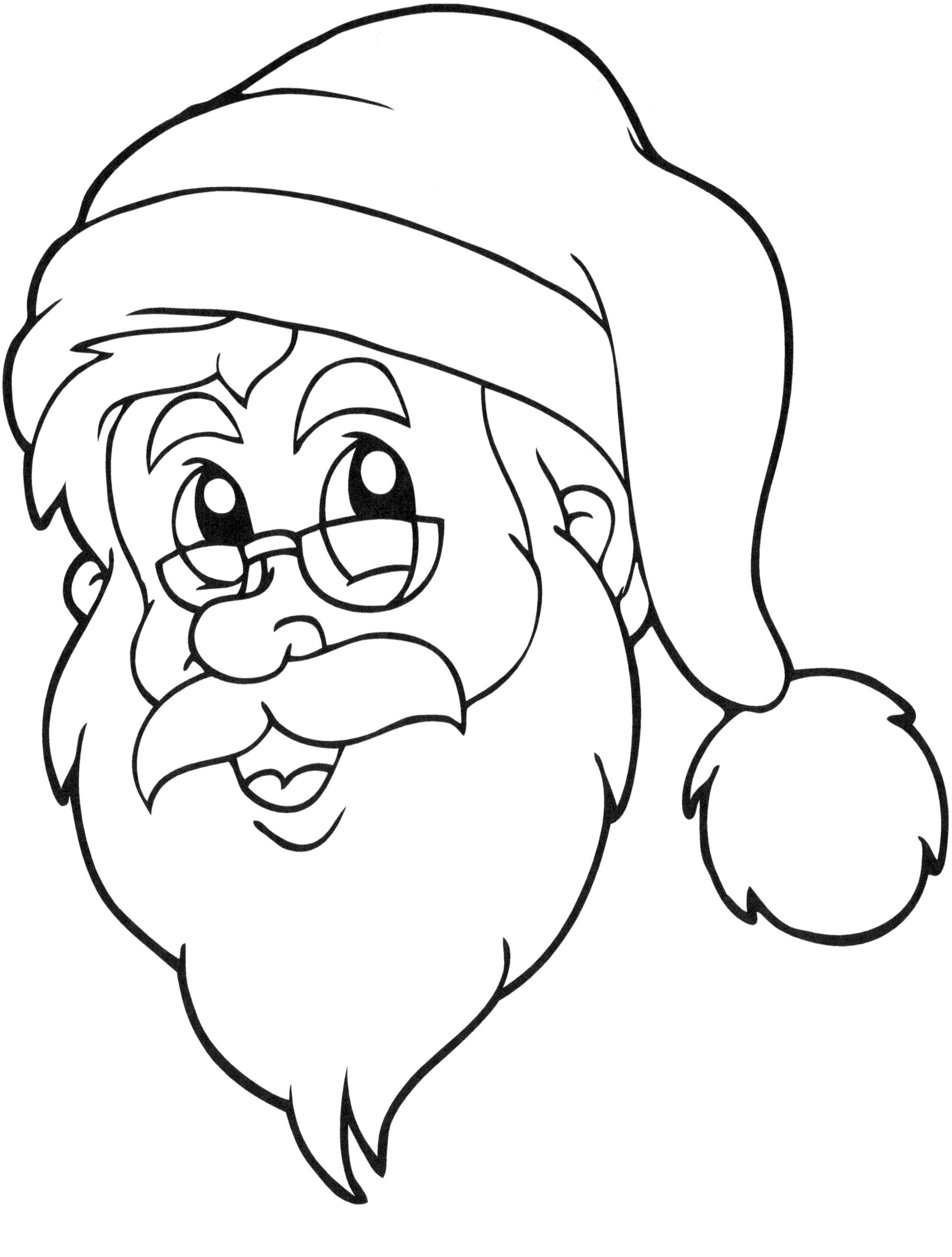

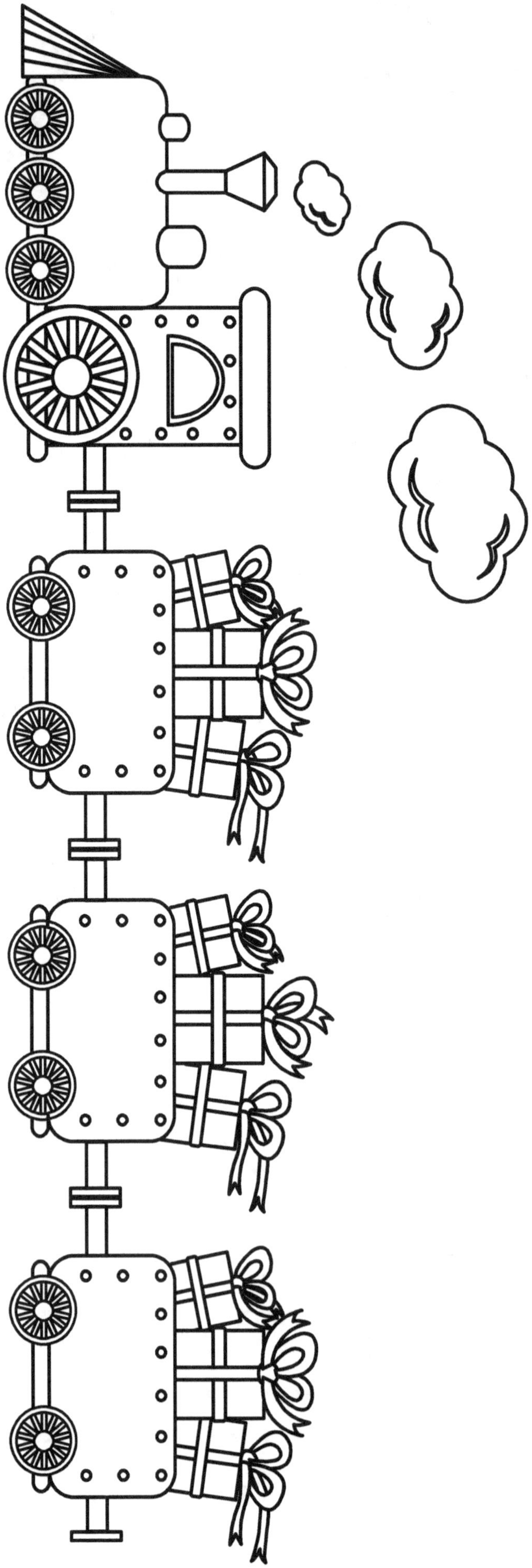

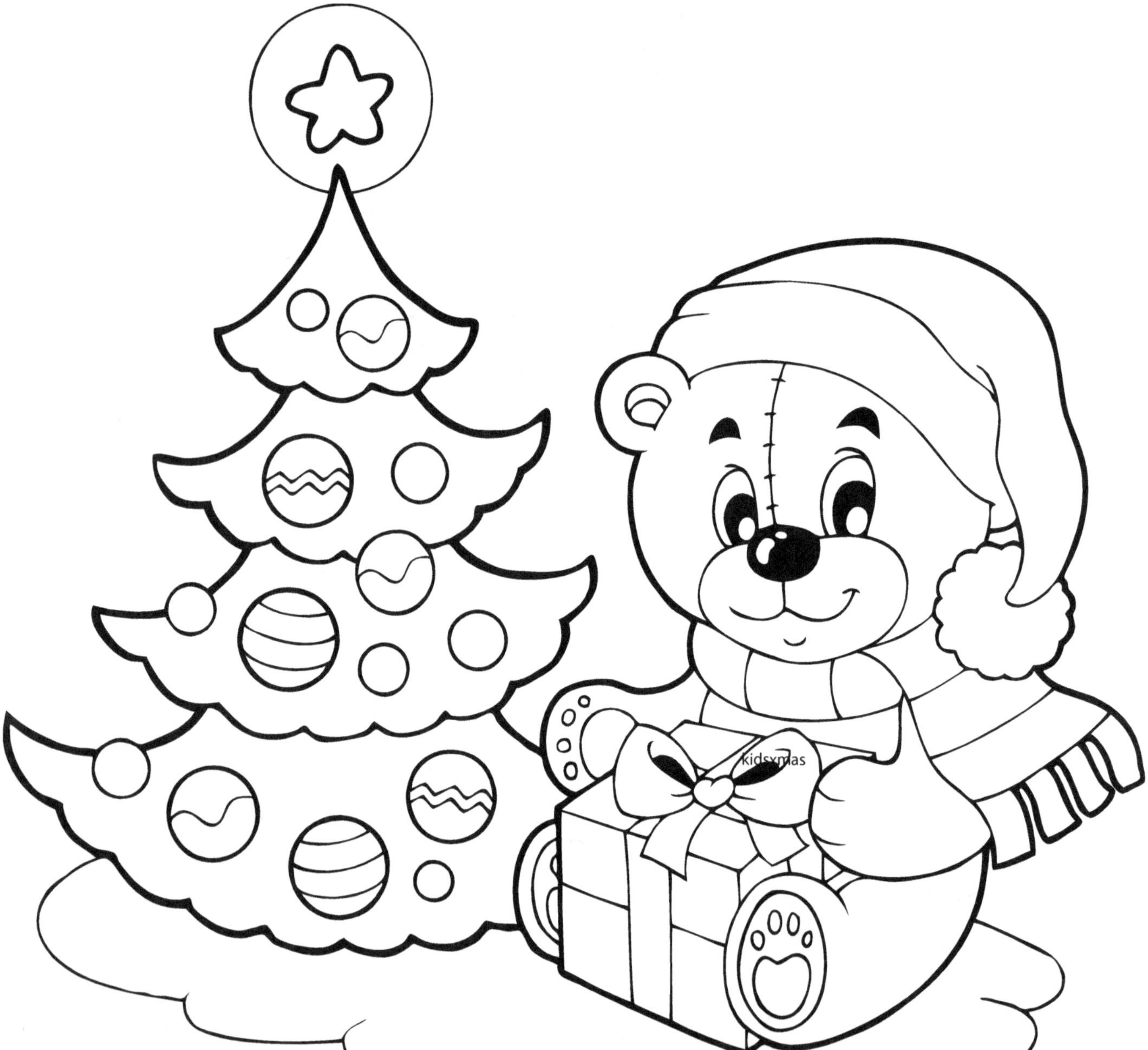
kidsxmas

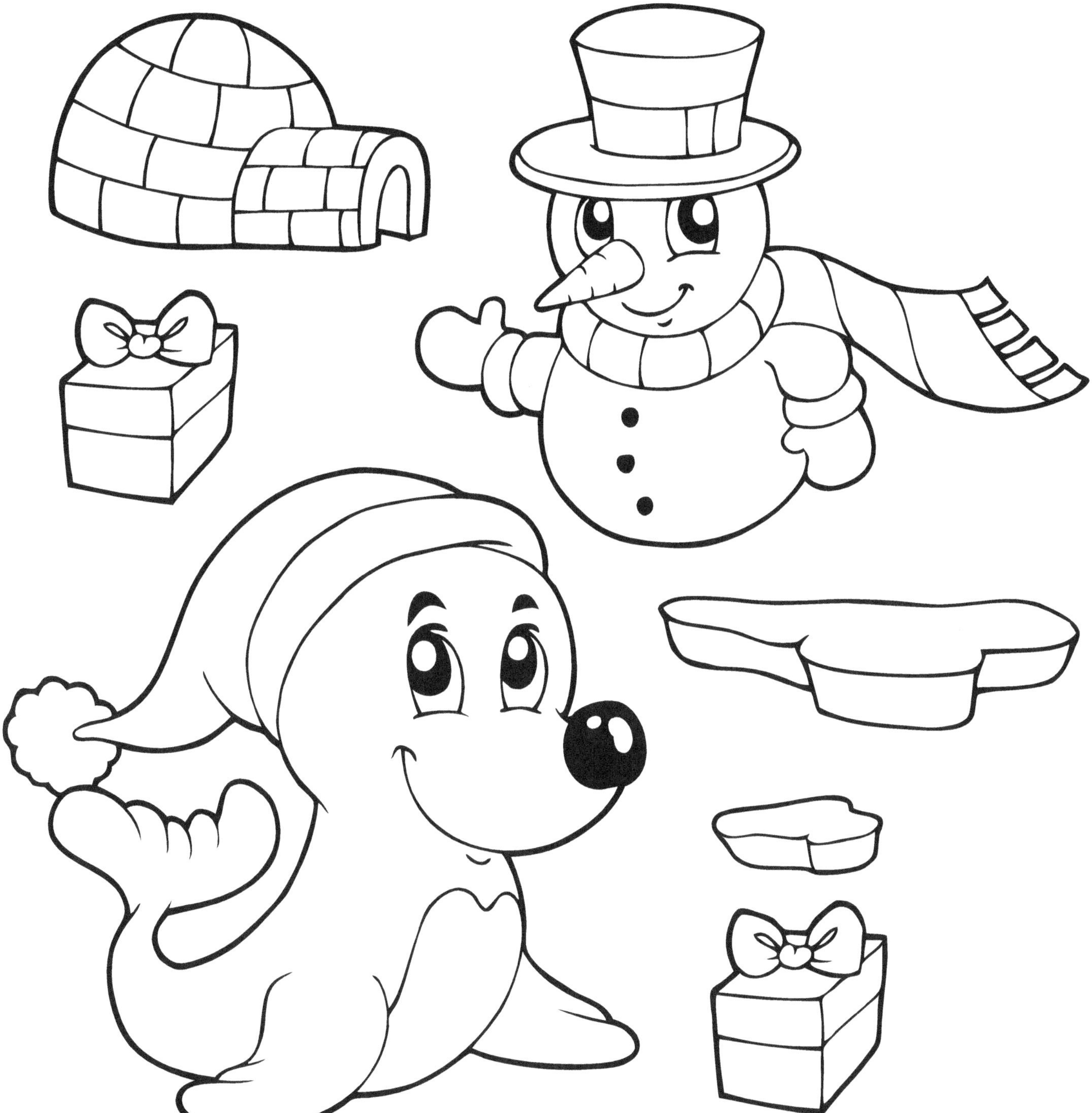

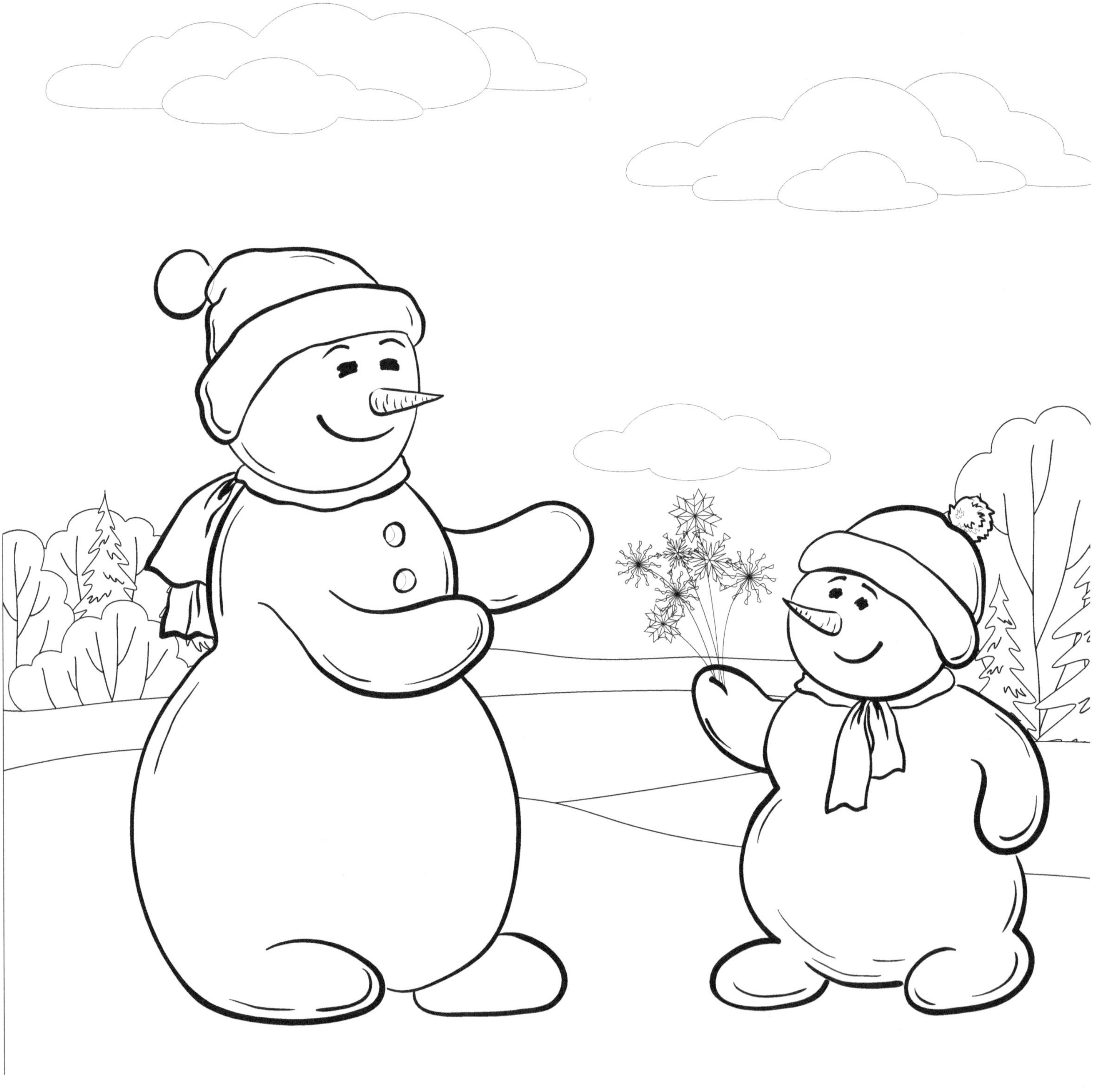

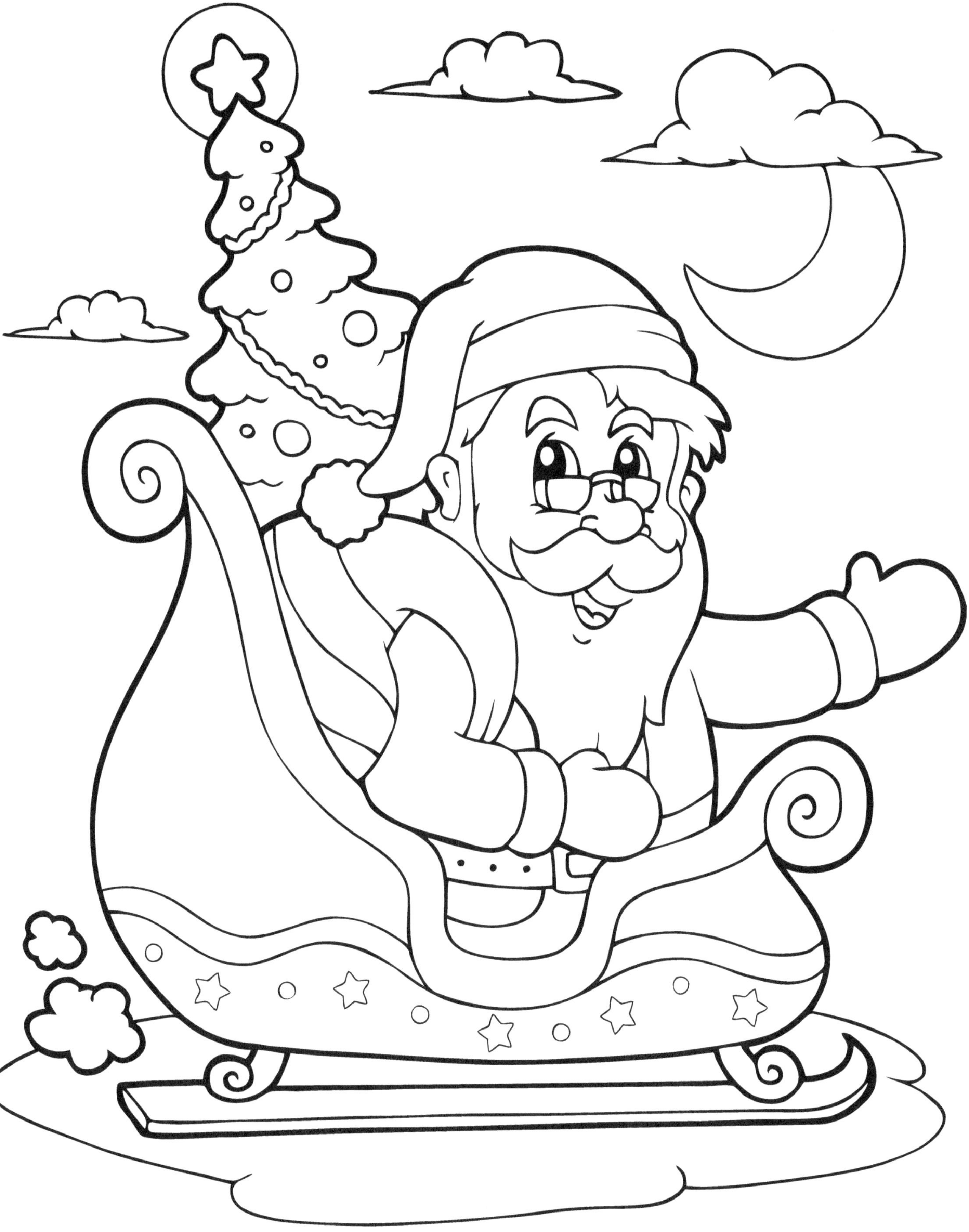

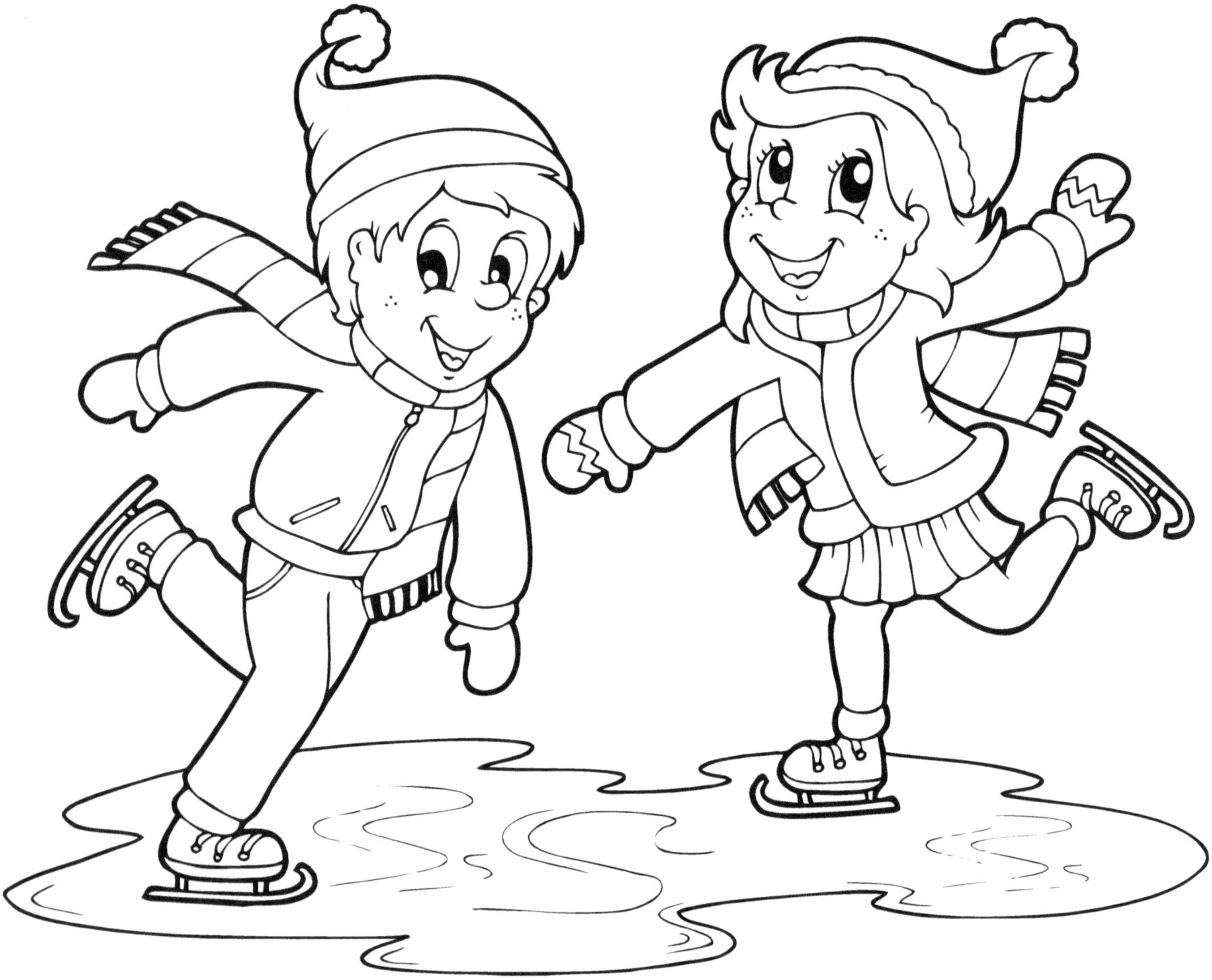

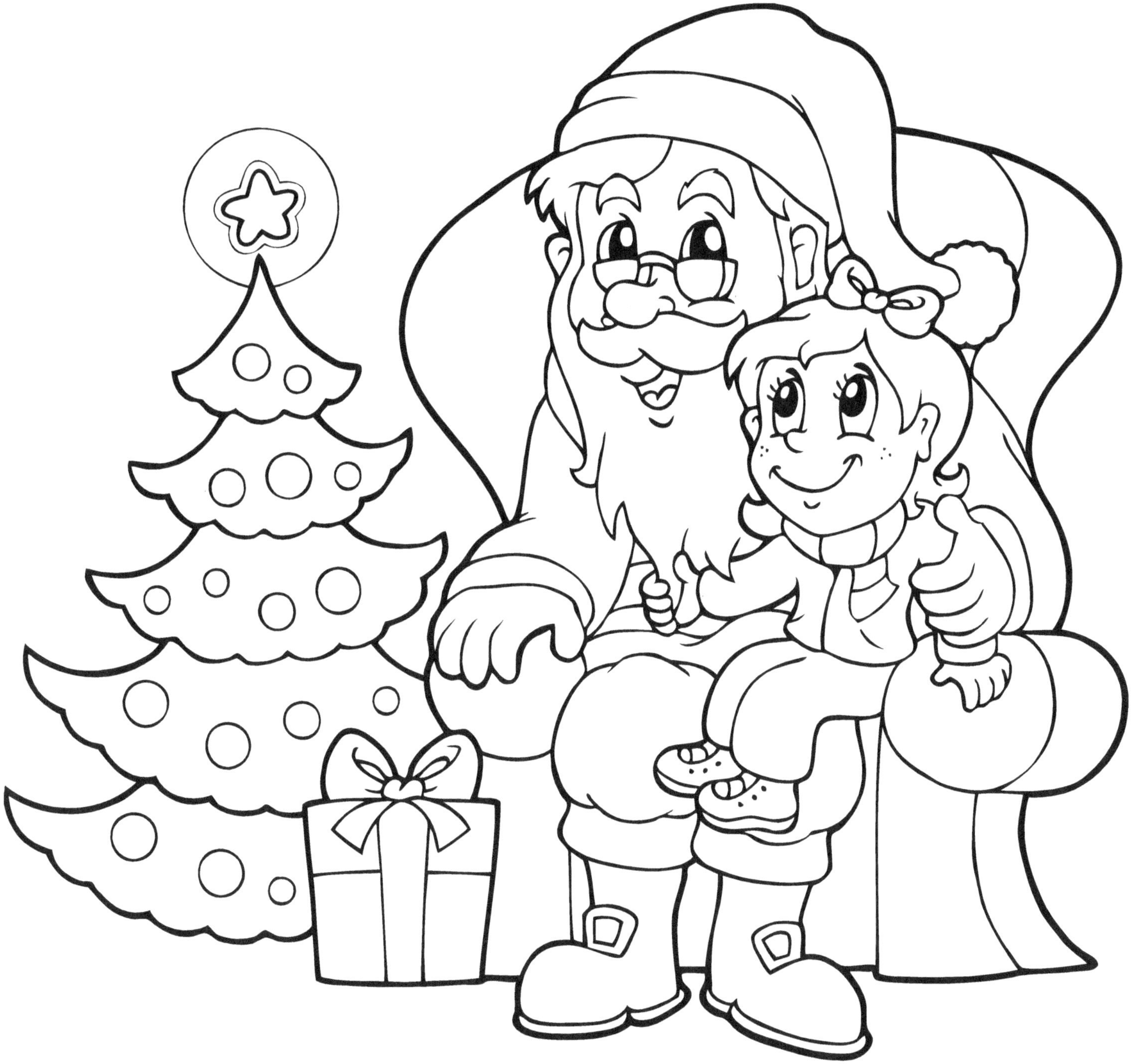

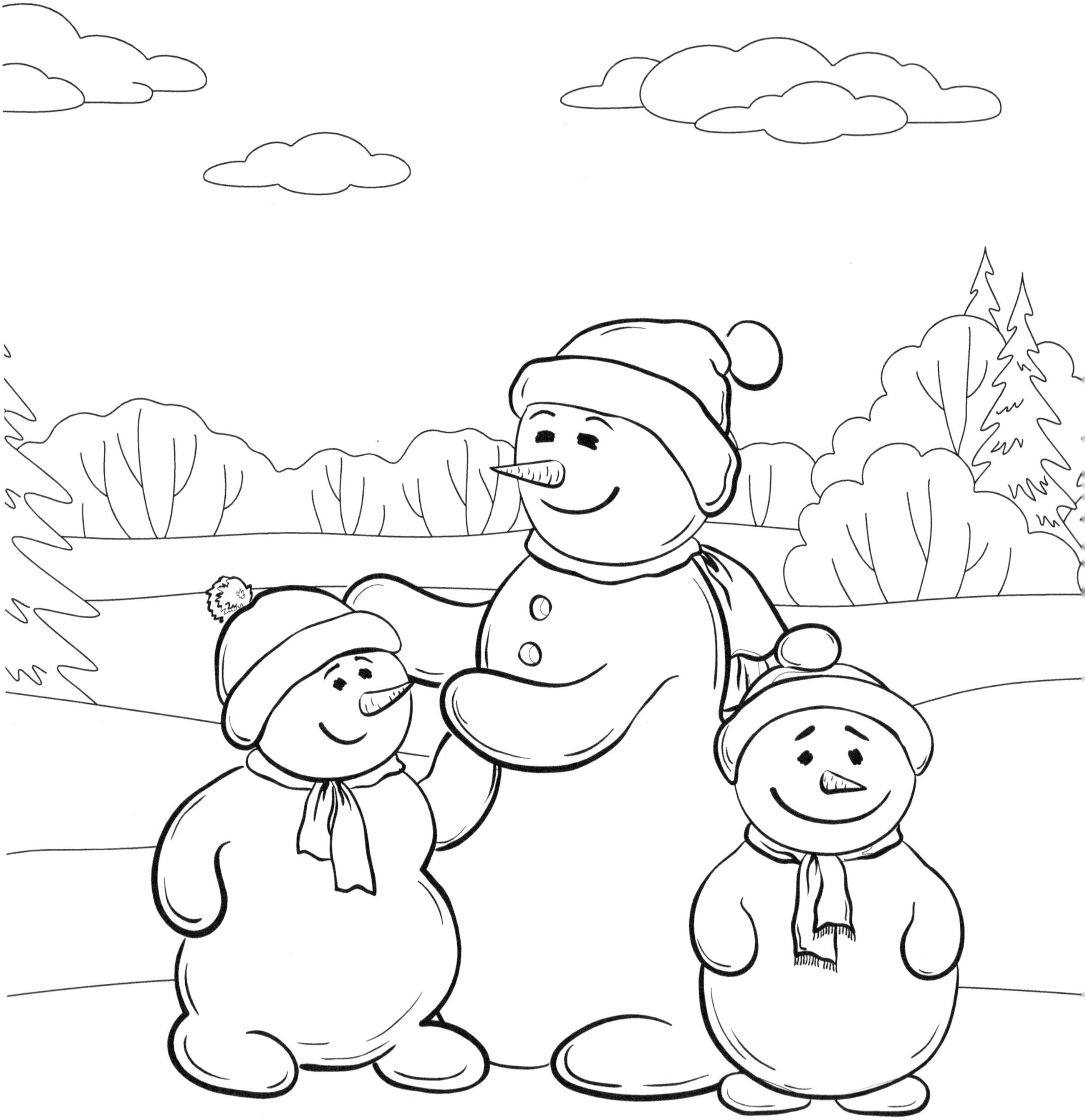

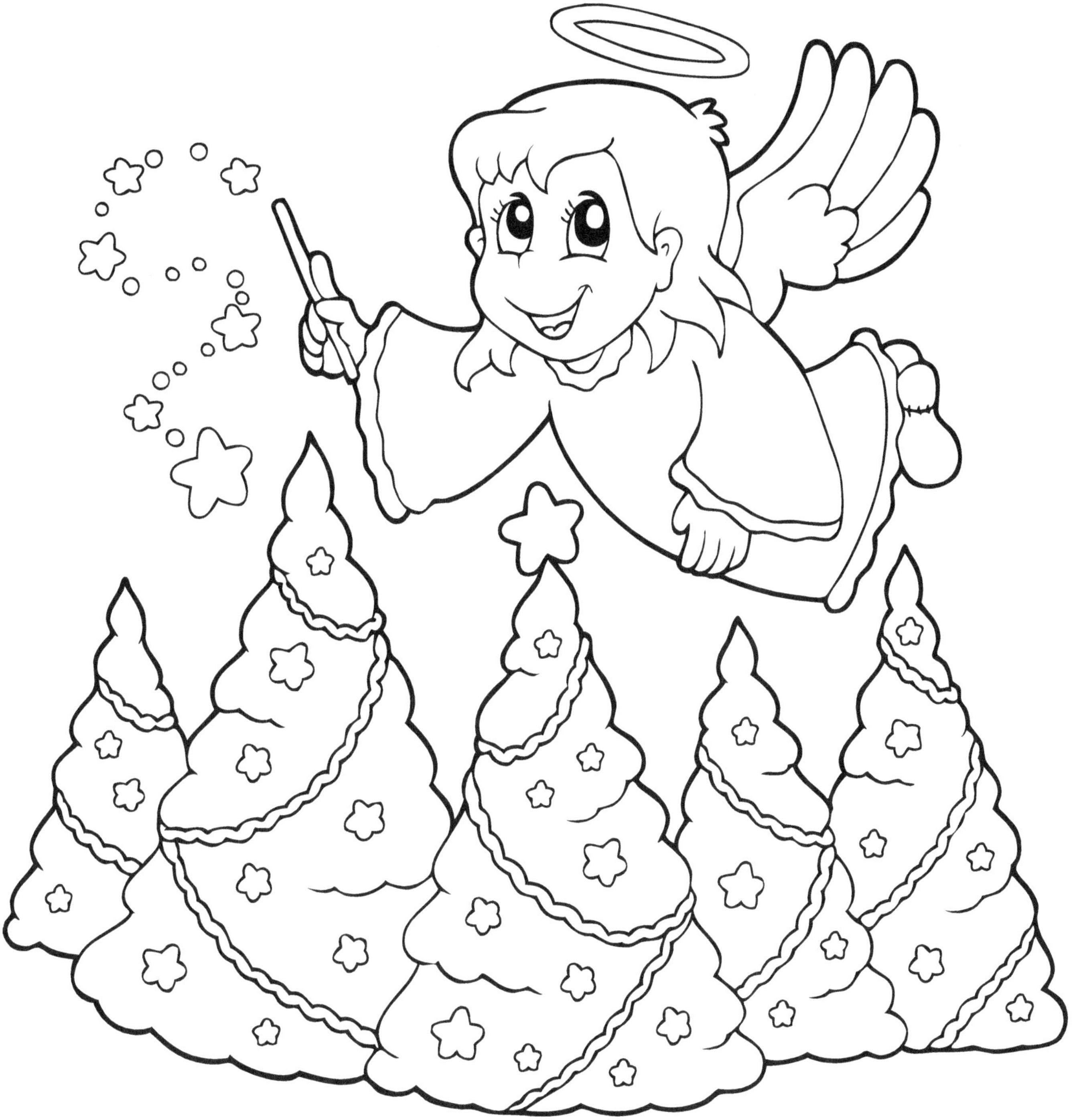

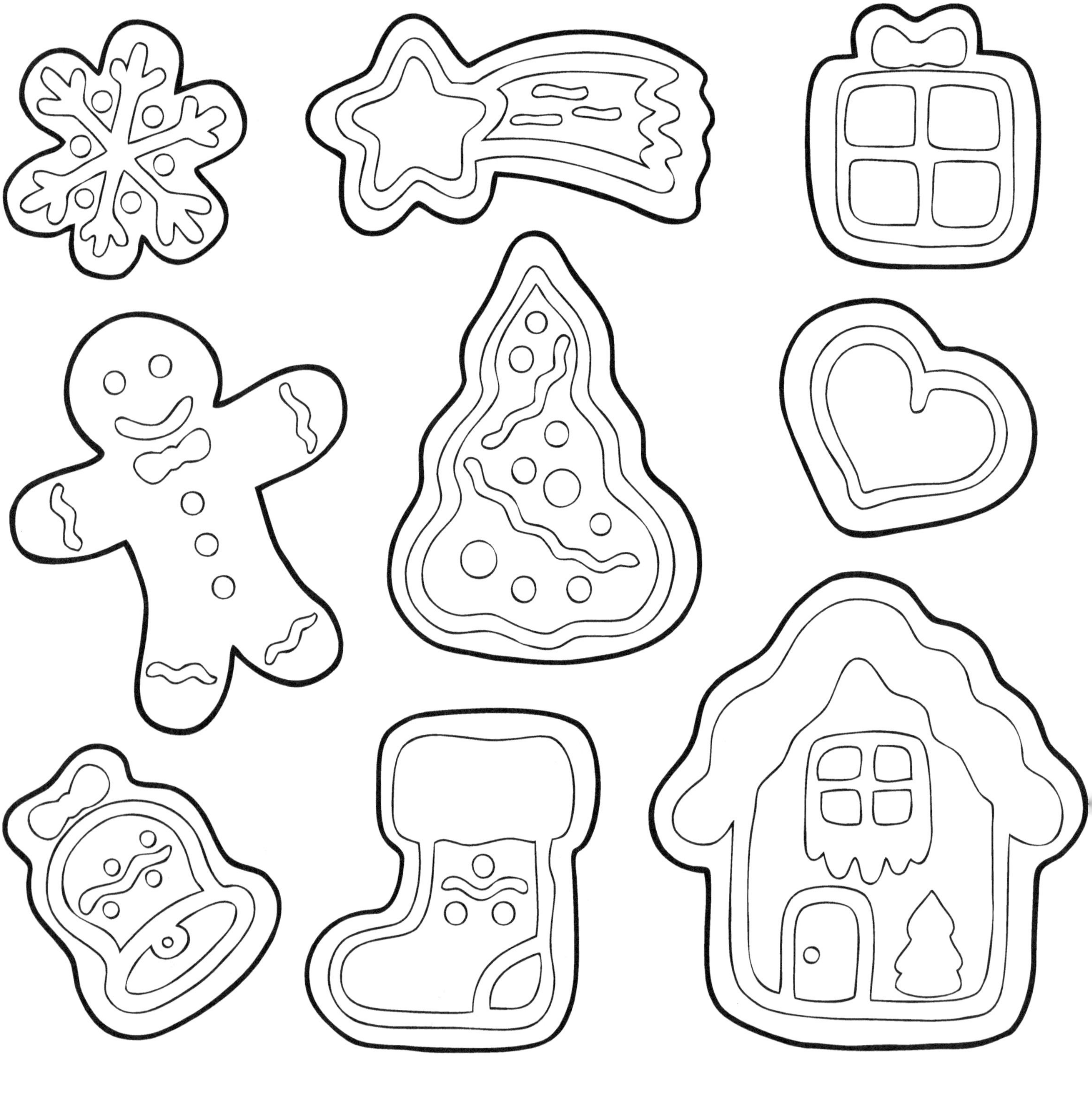

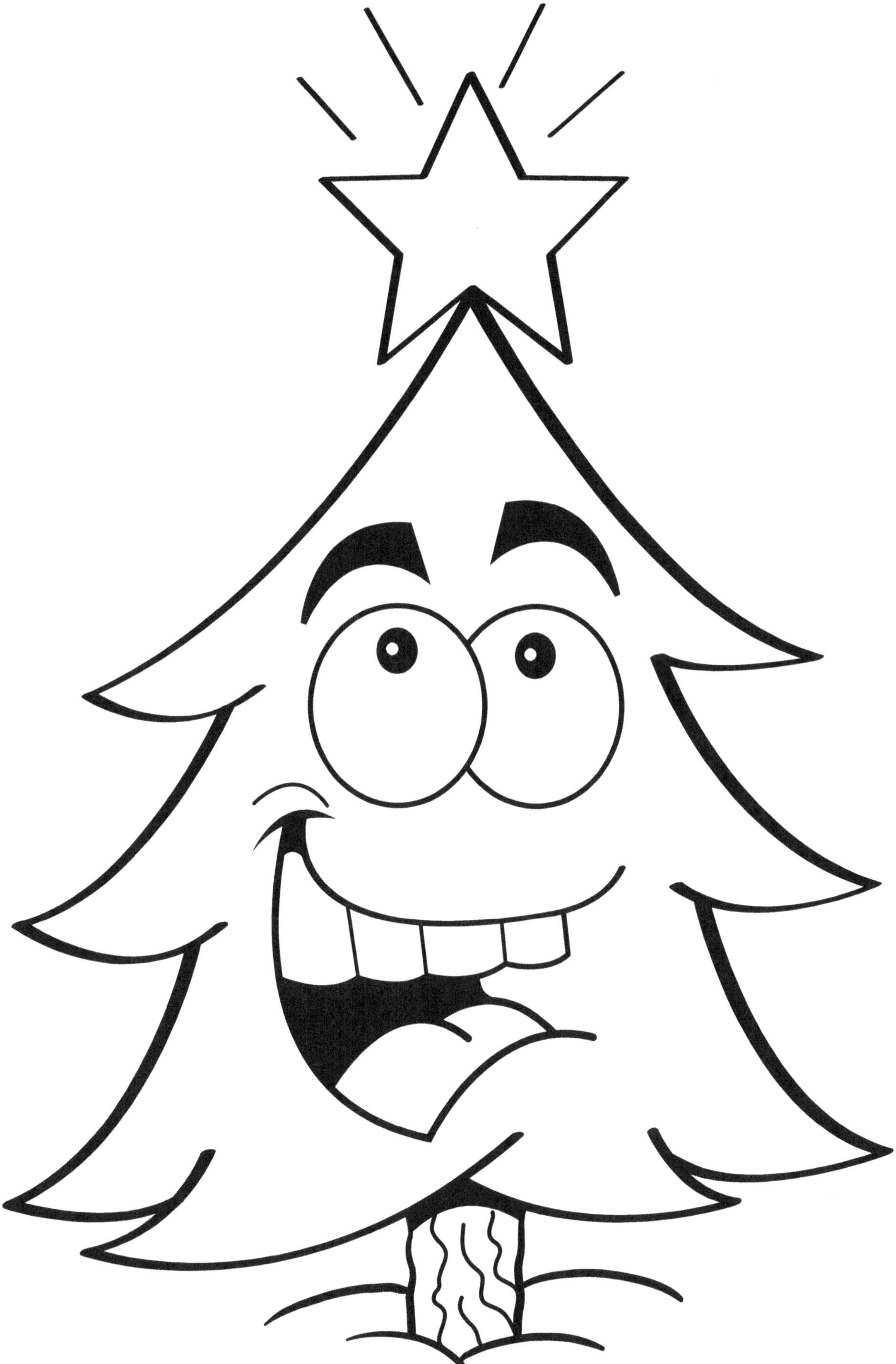

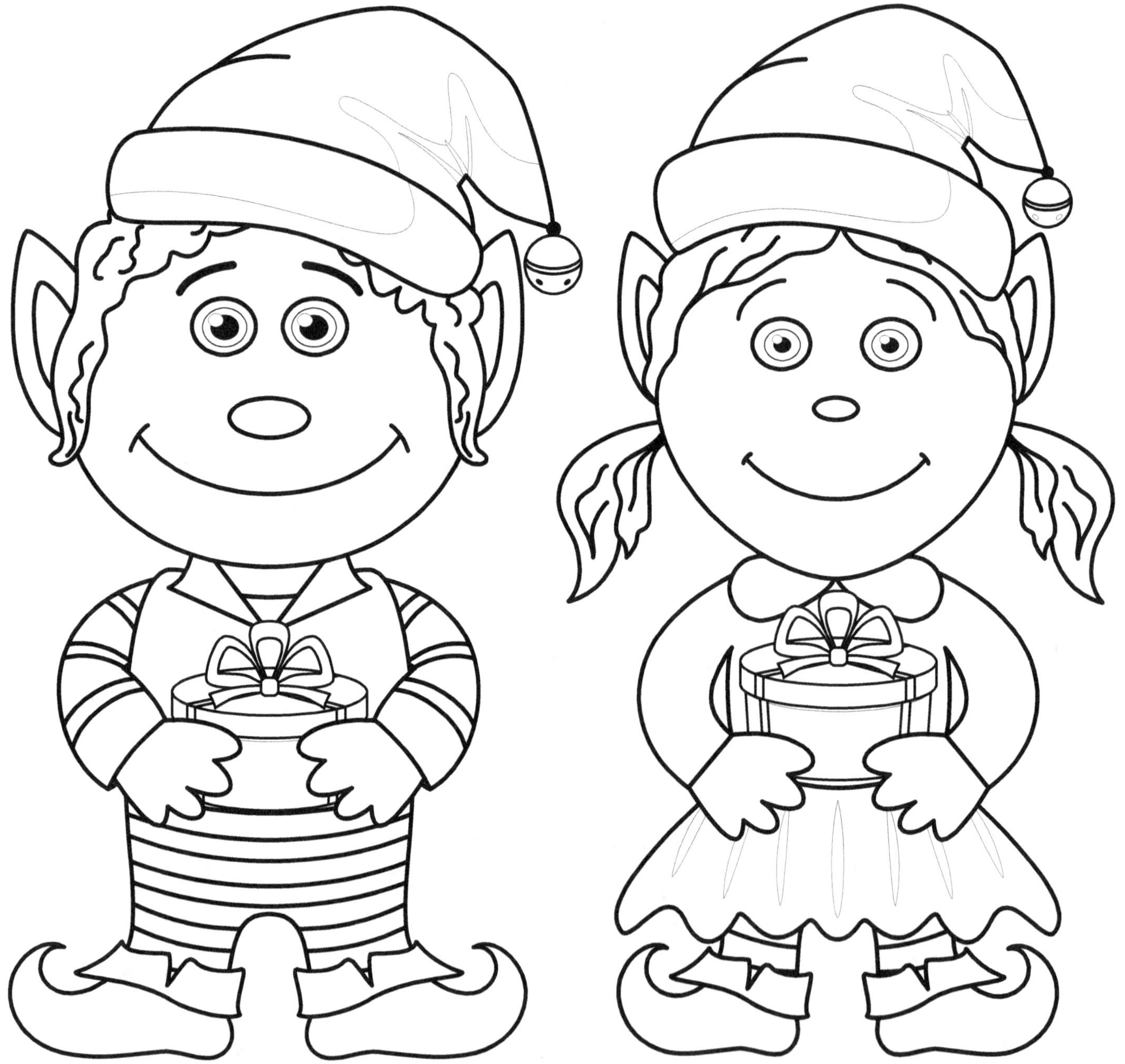

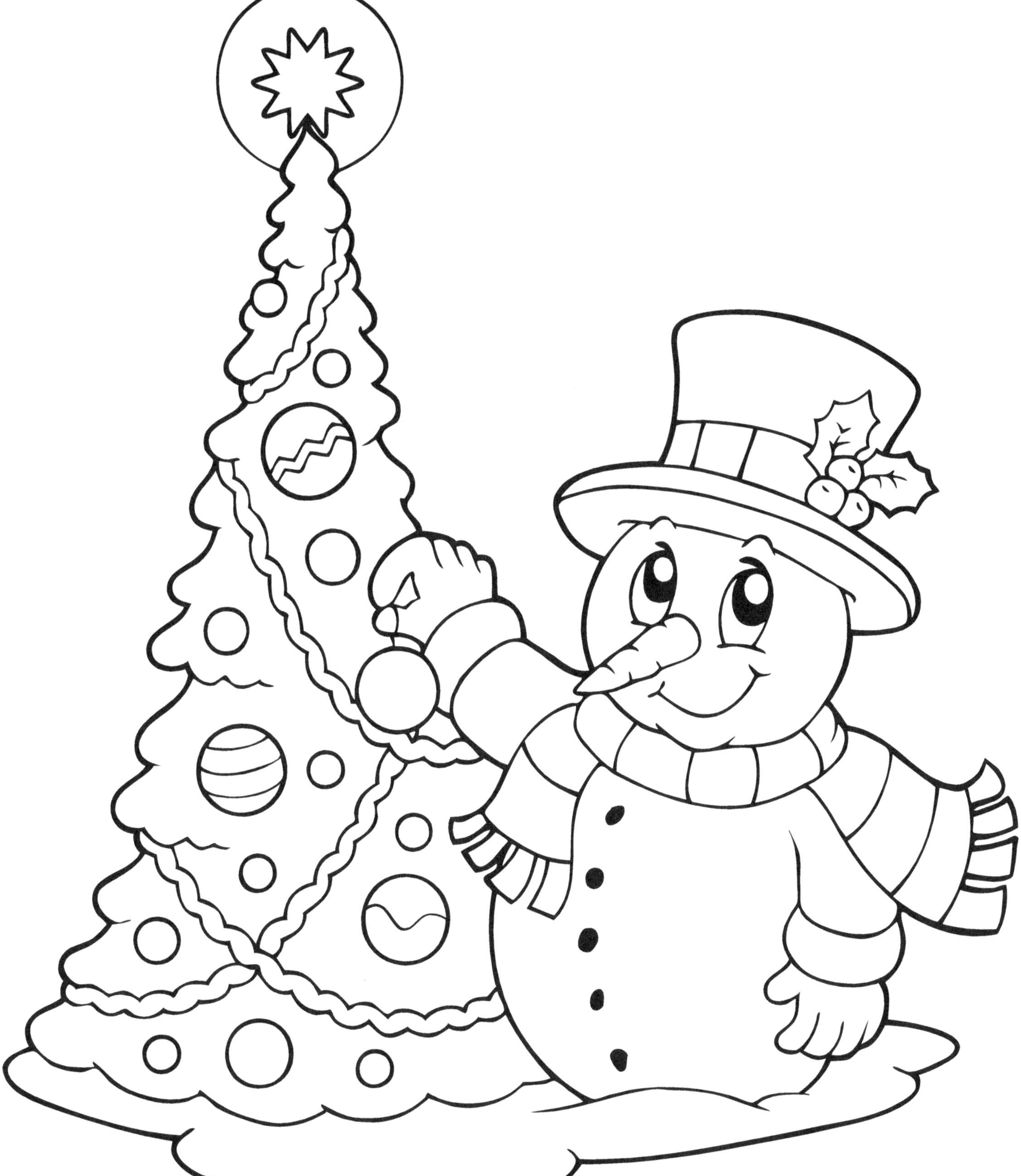

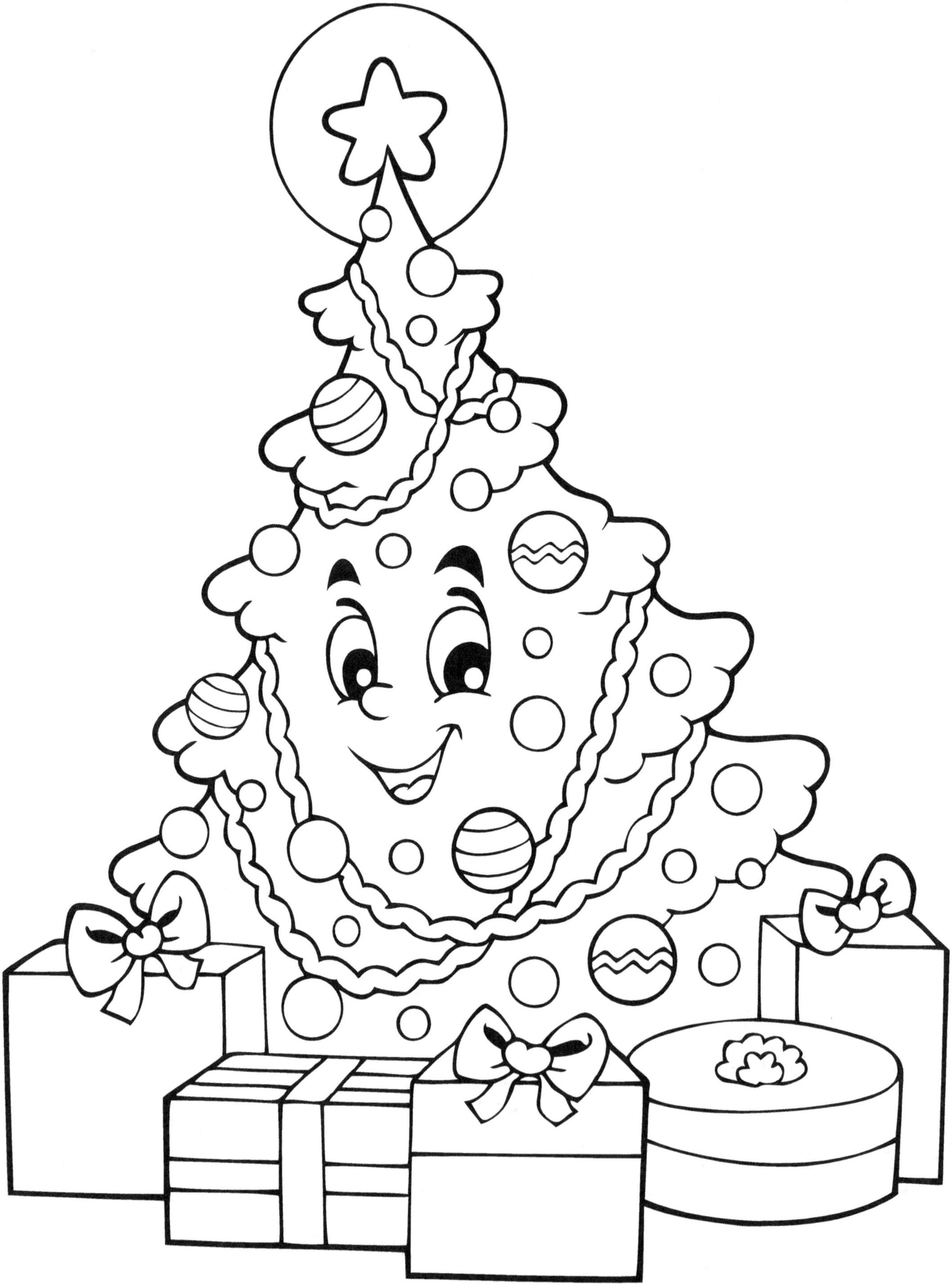

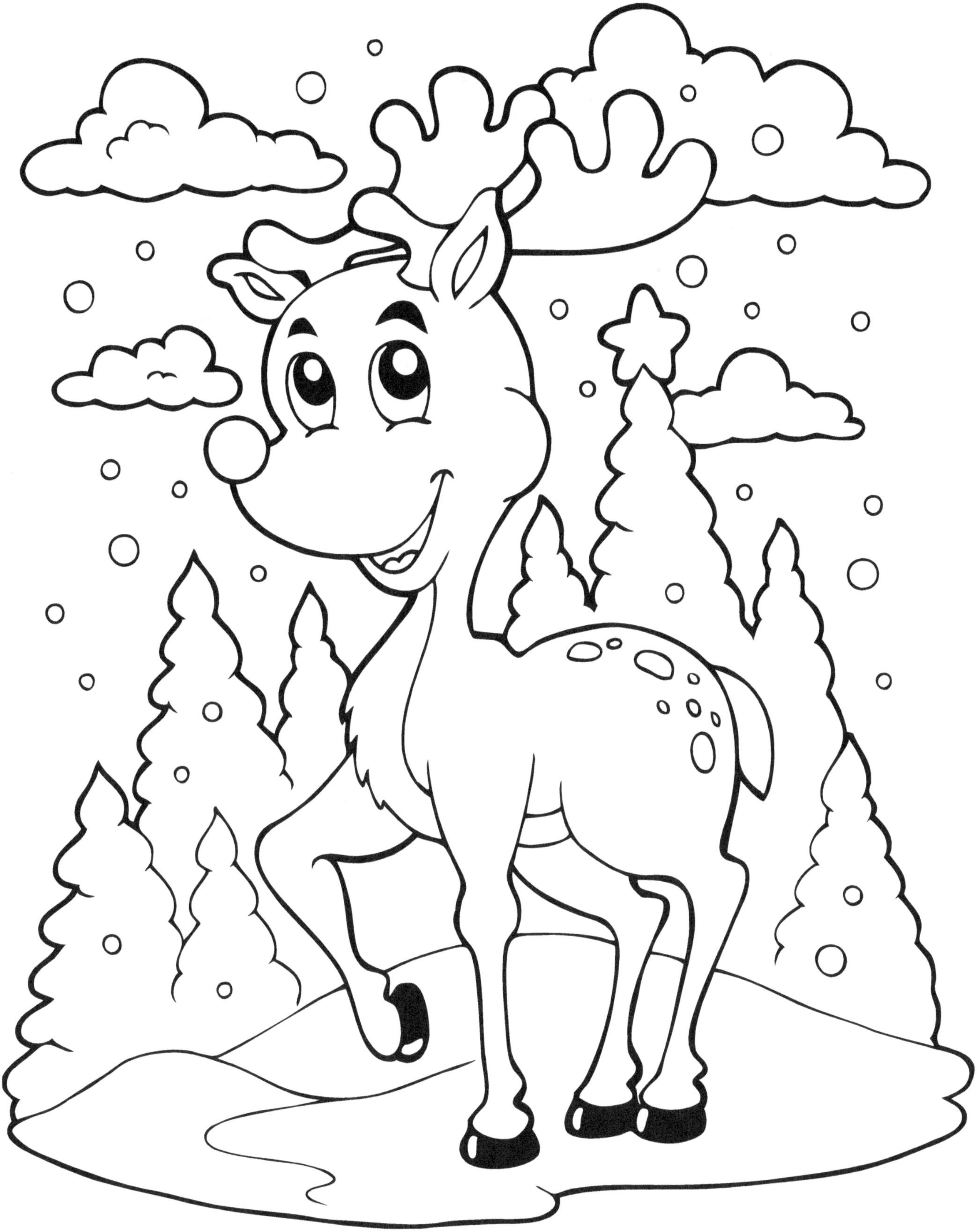

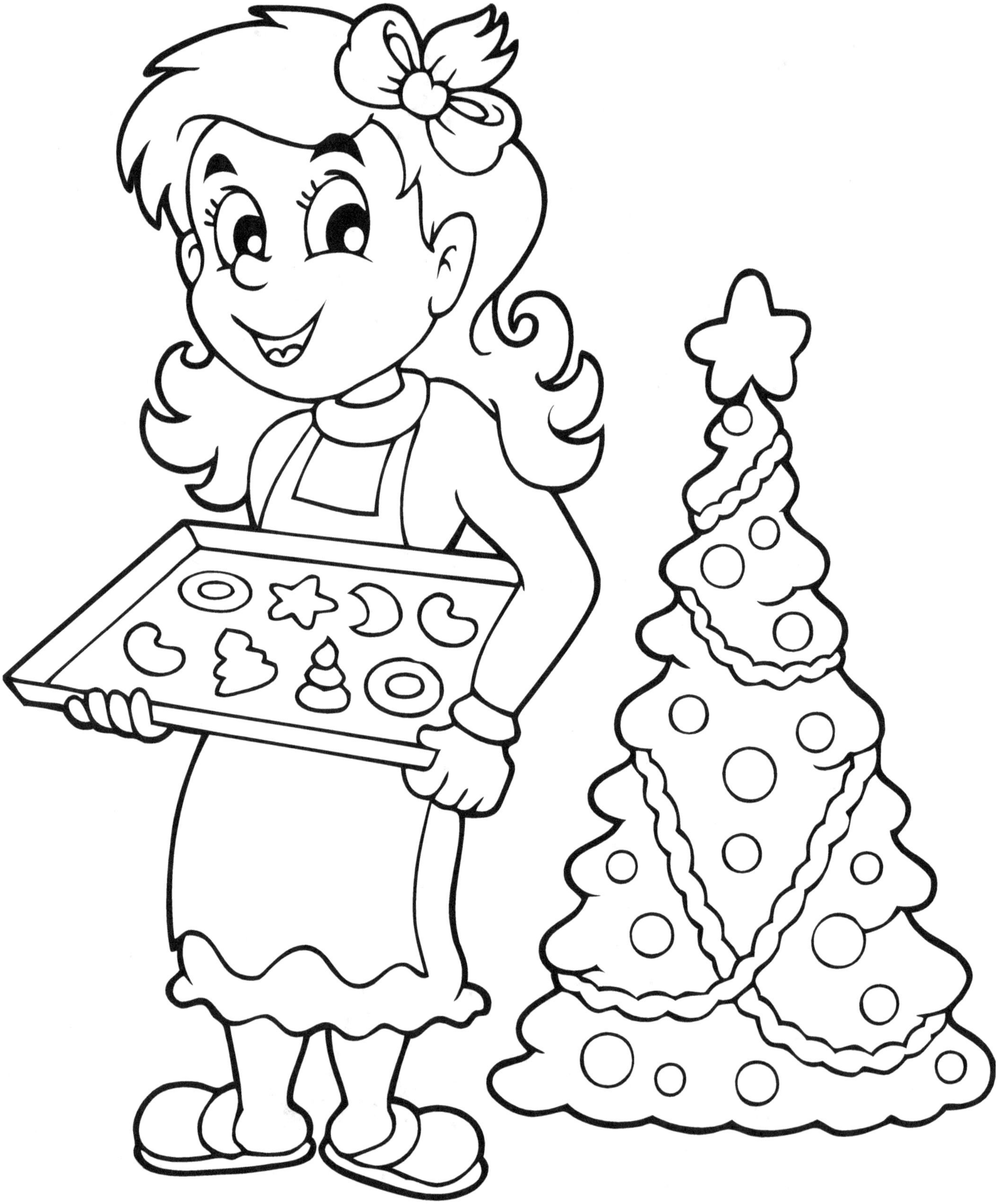

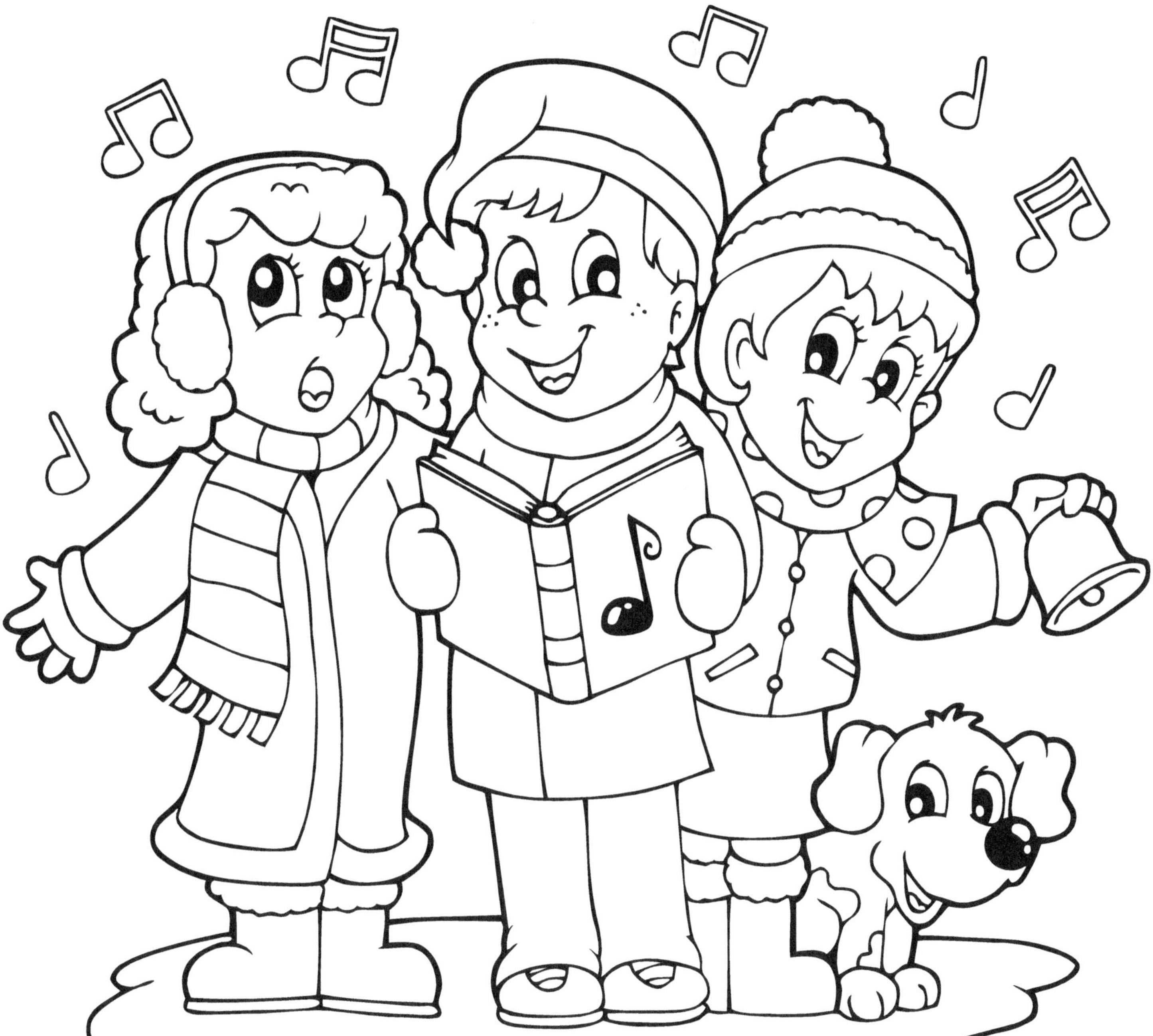

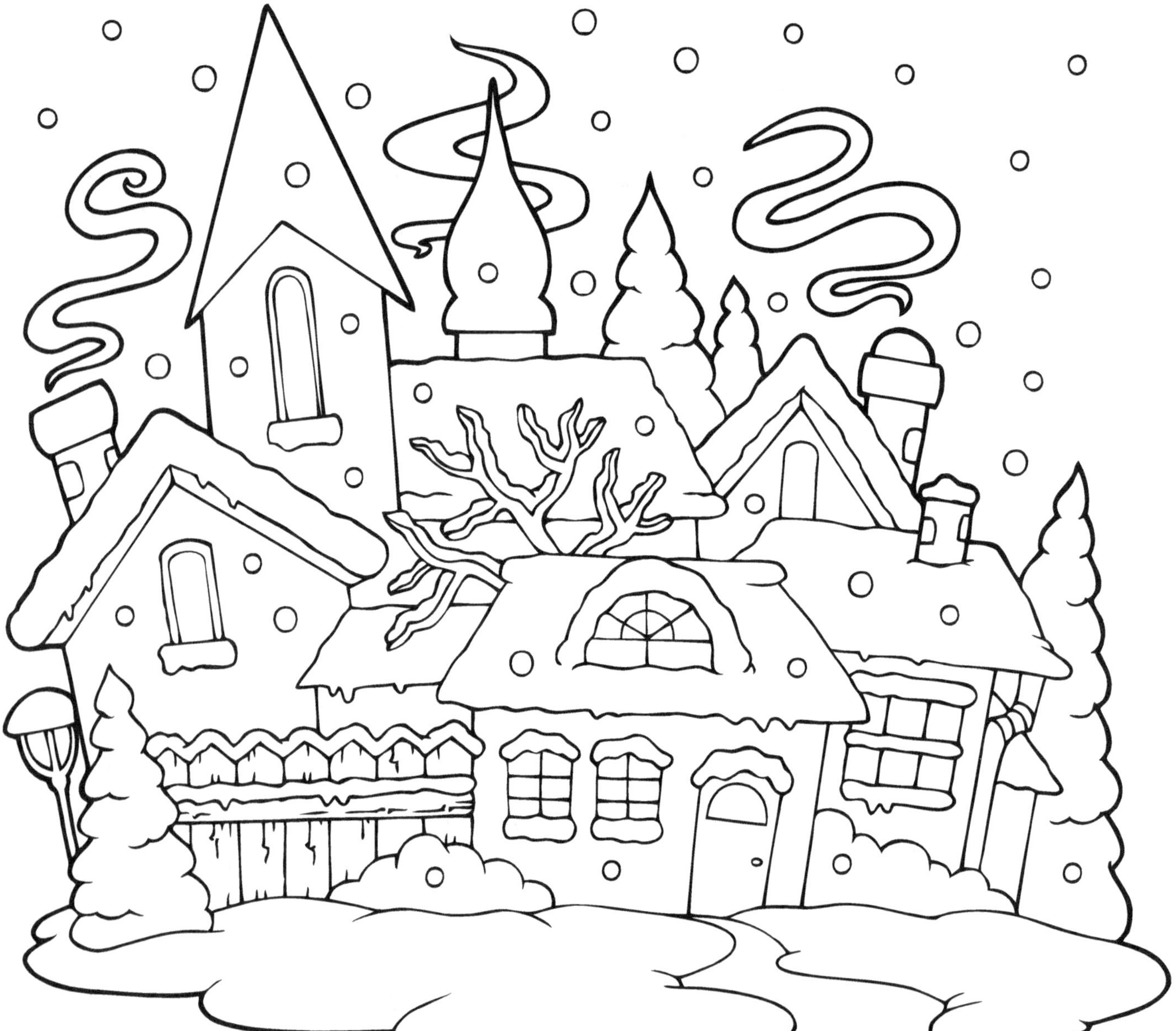

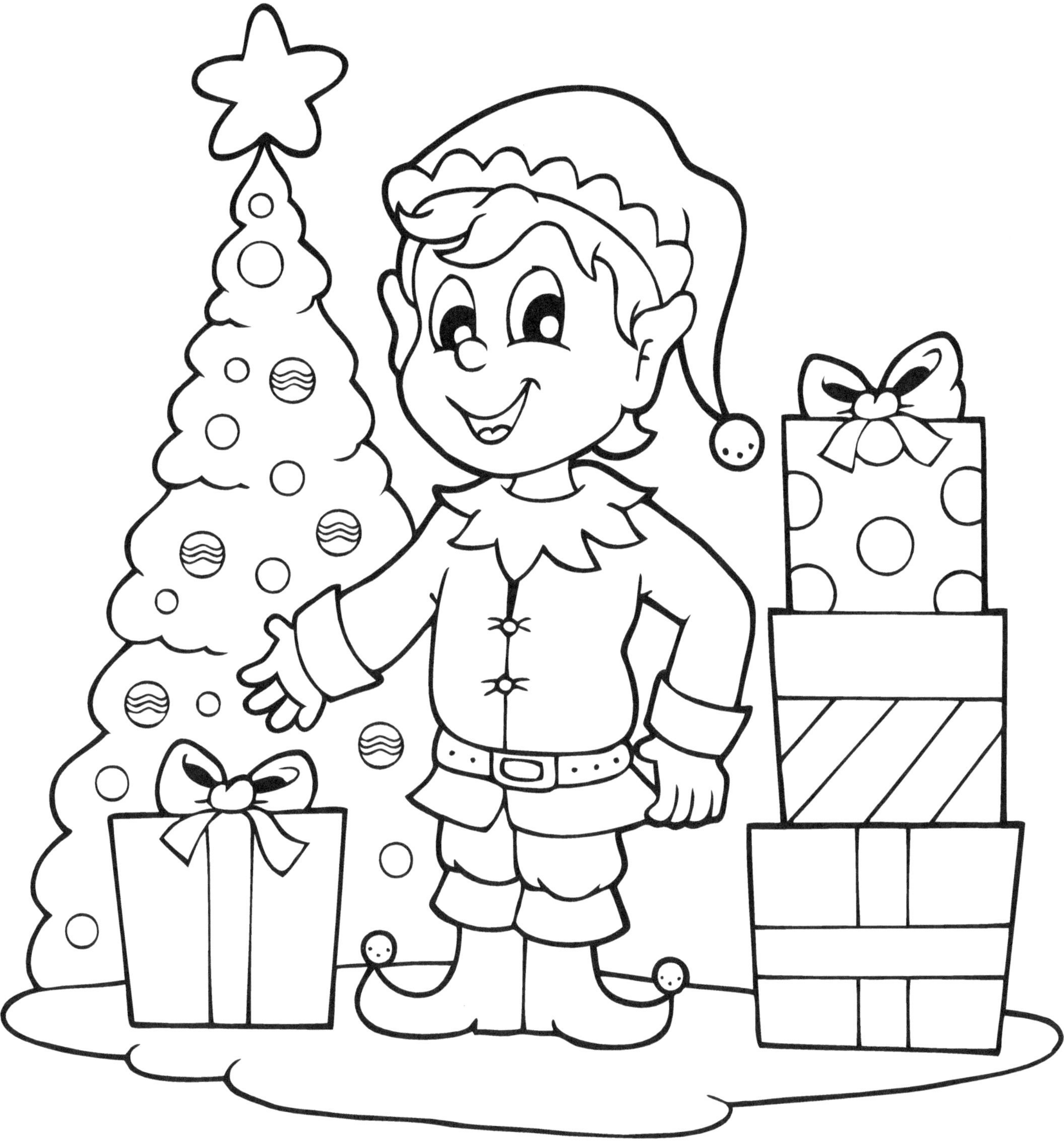

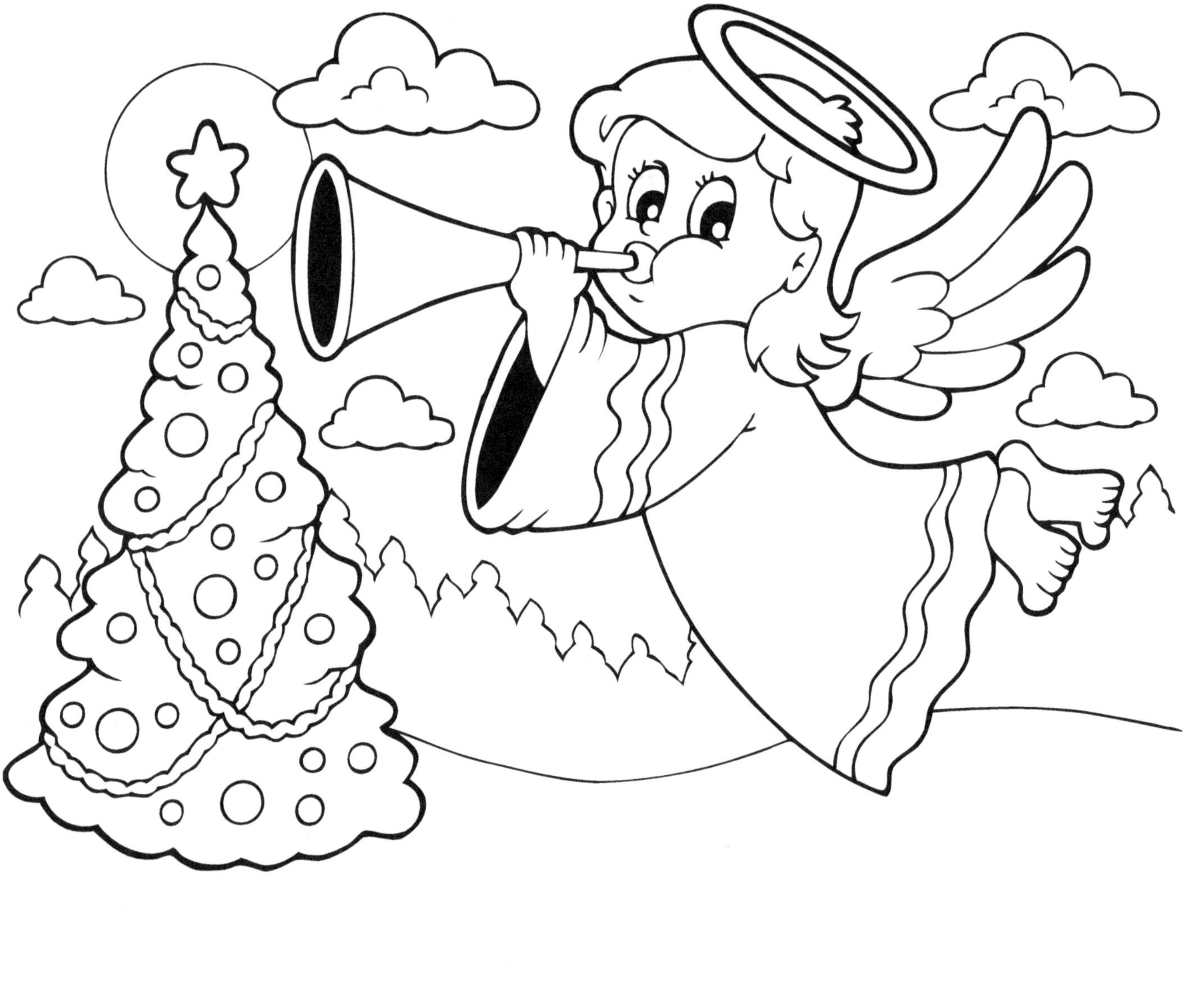

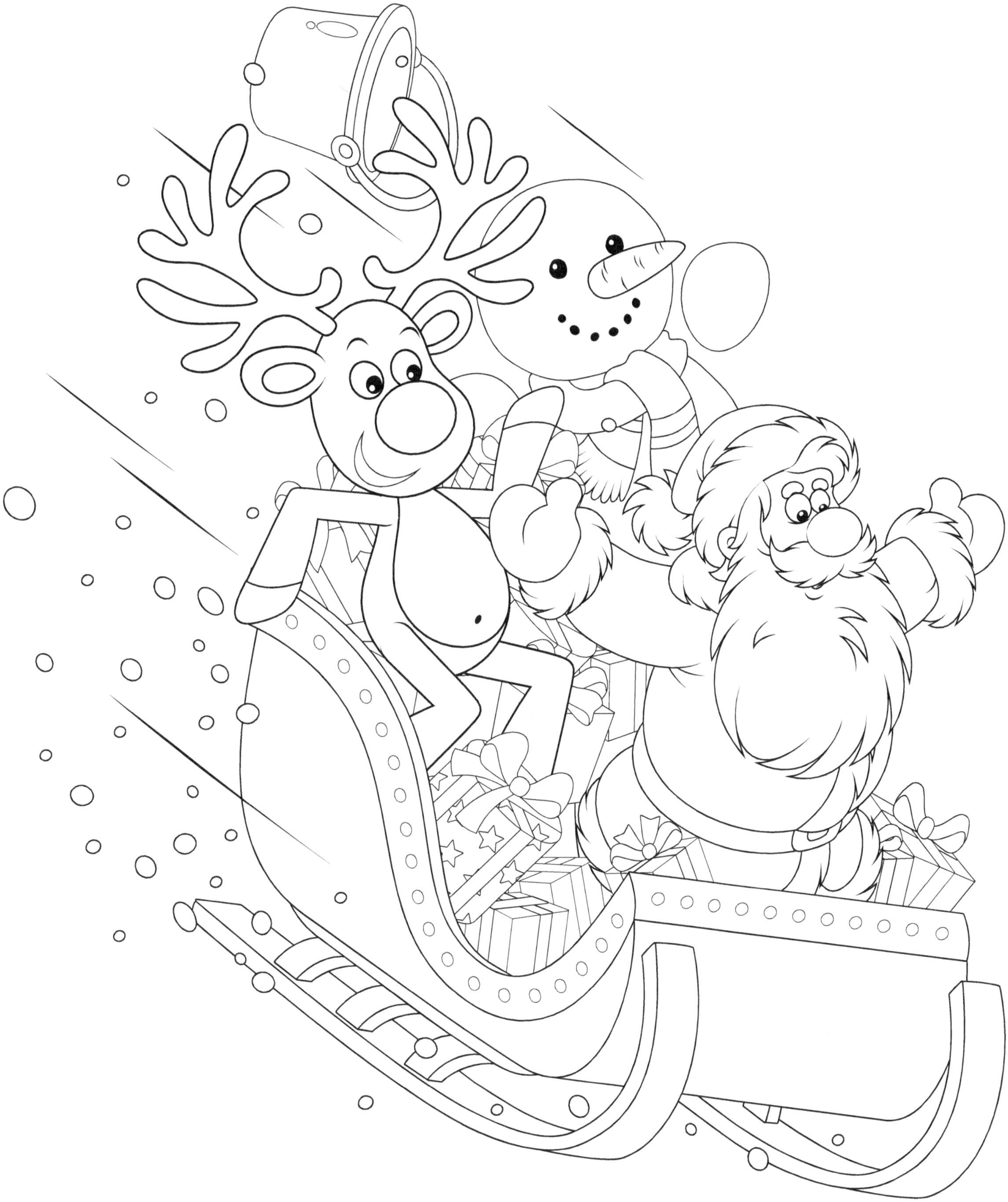

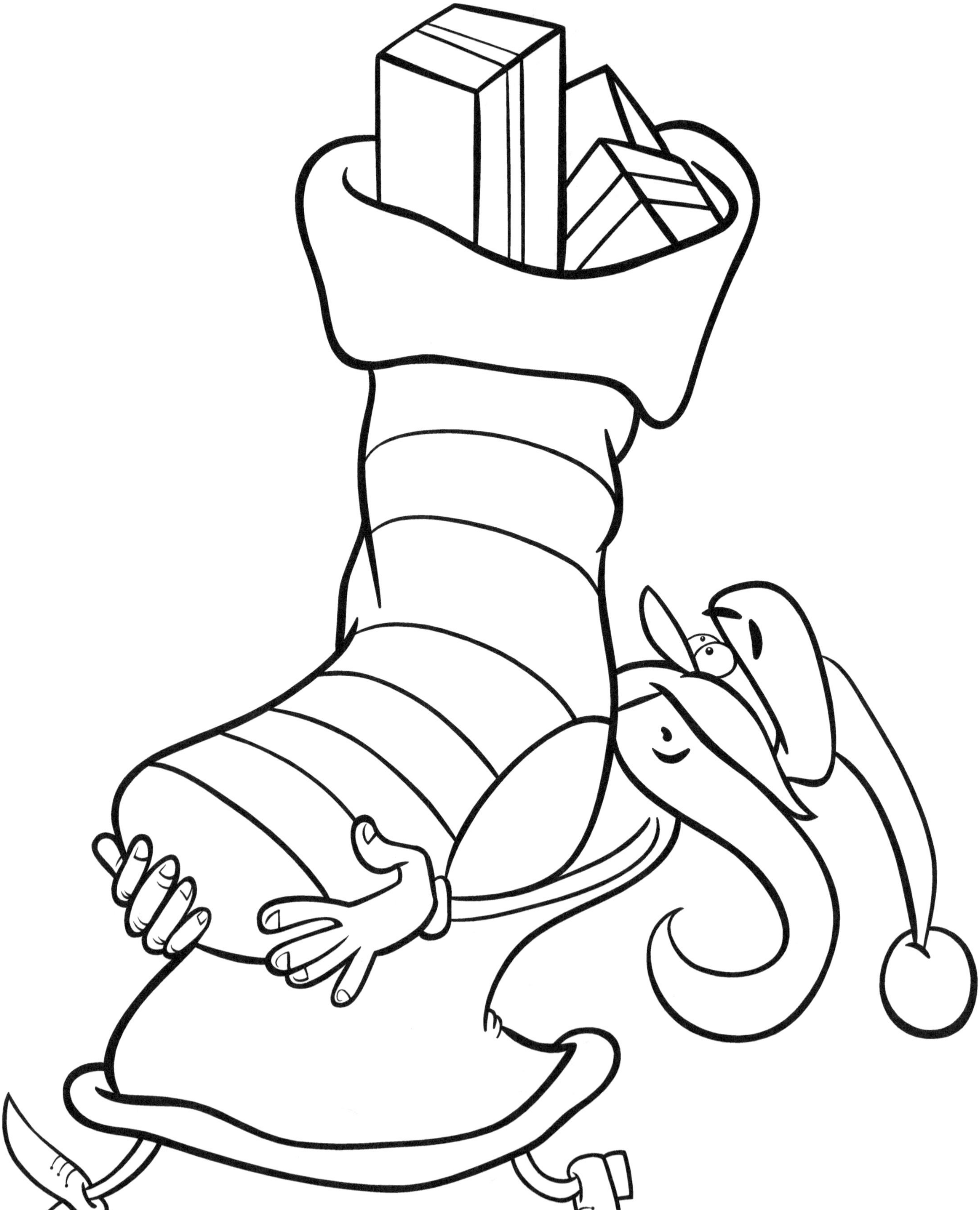

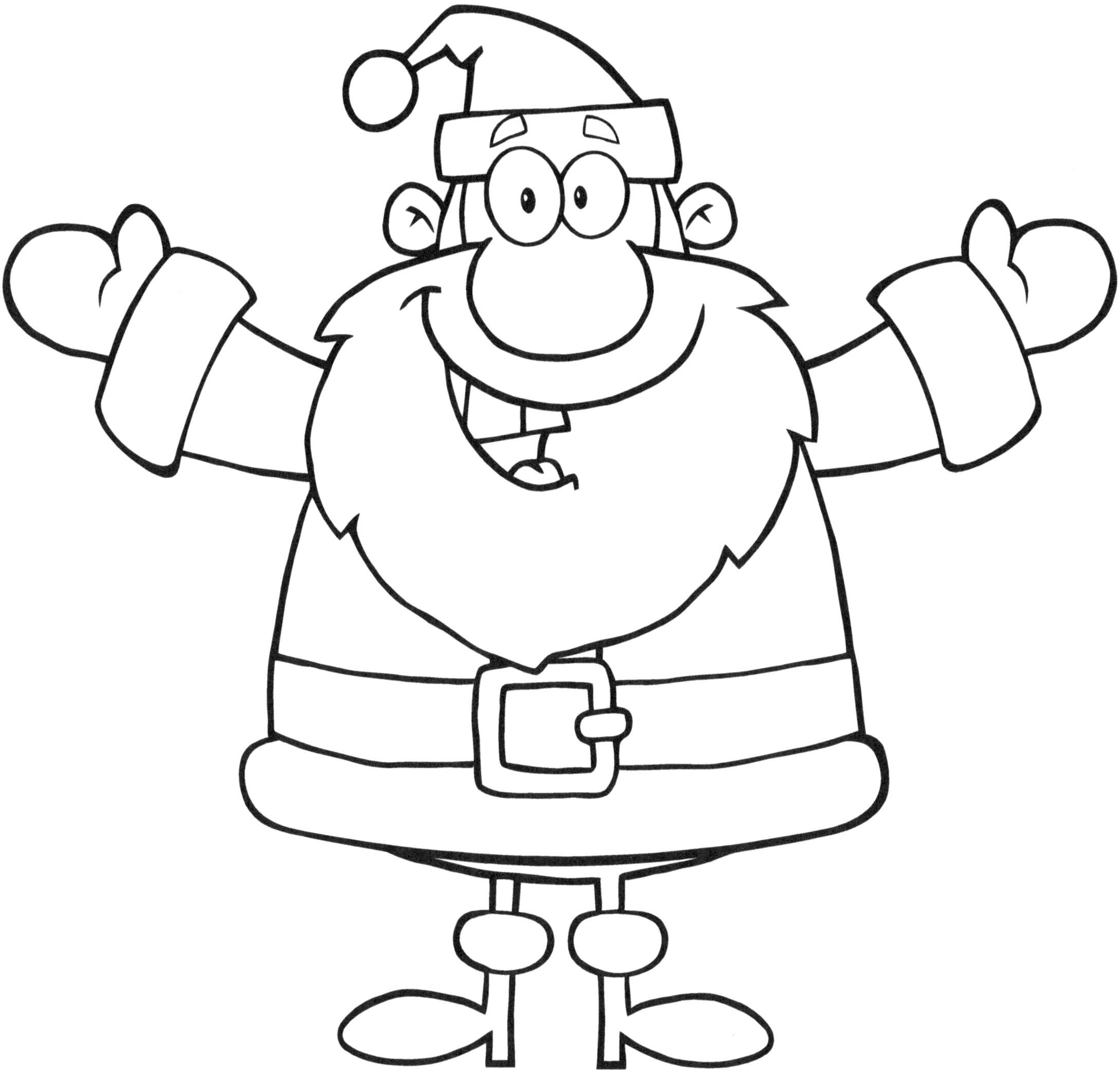

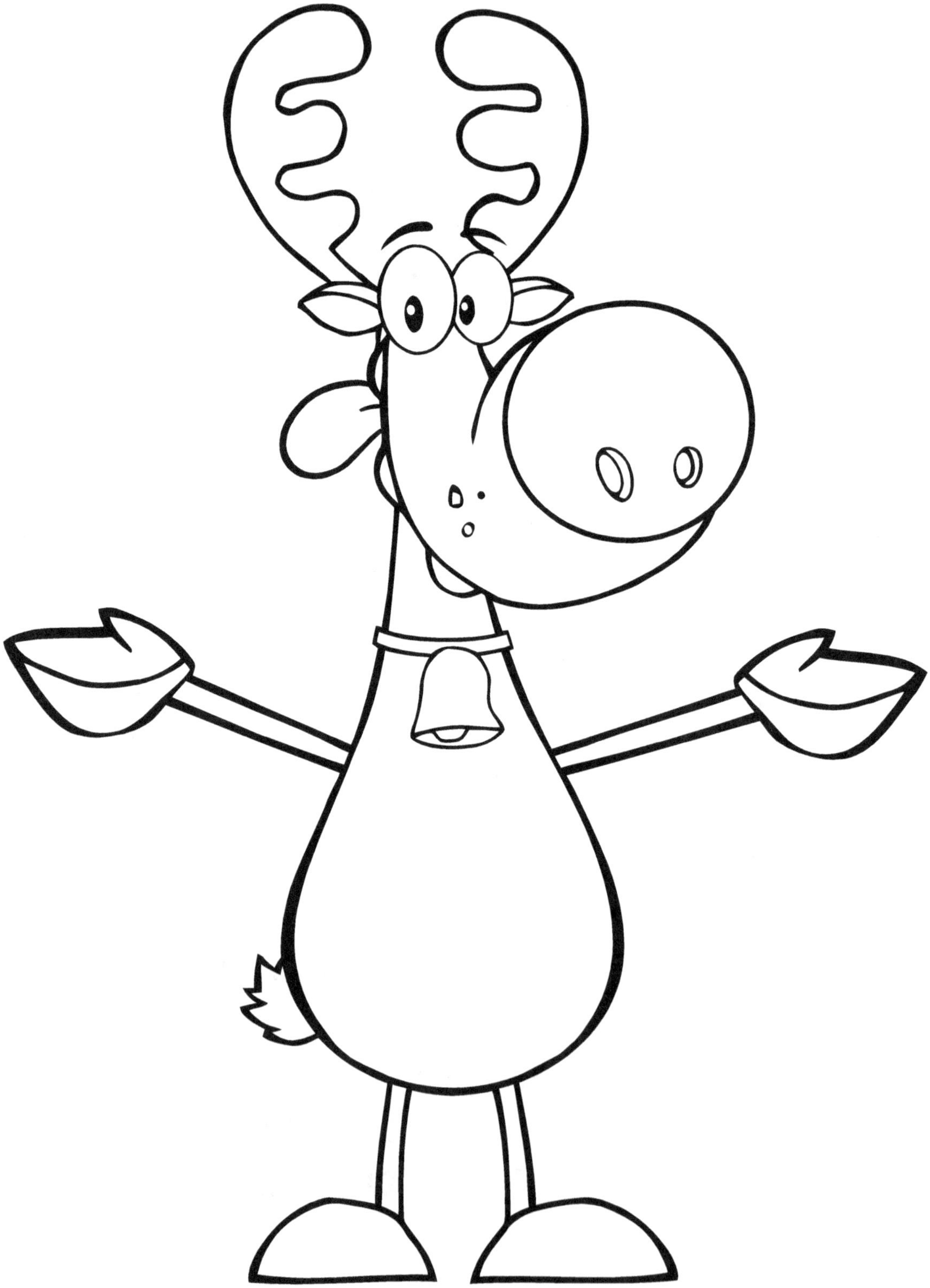

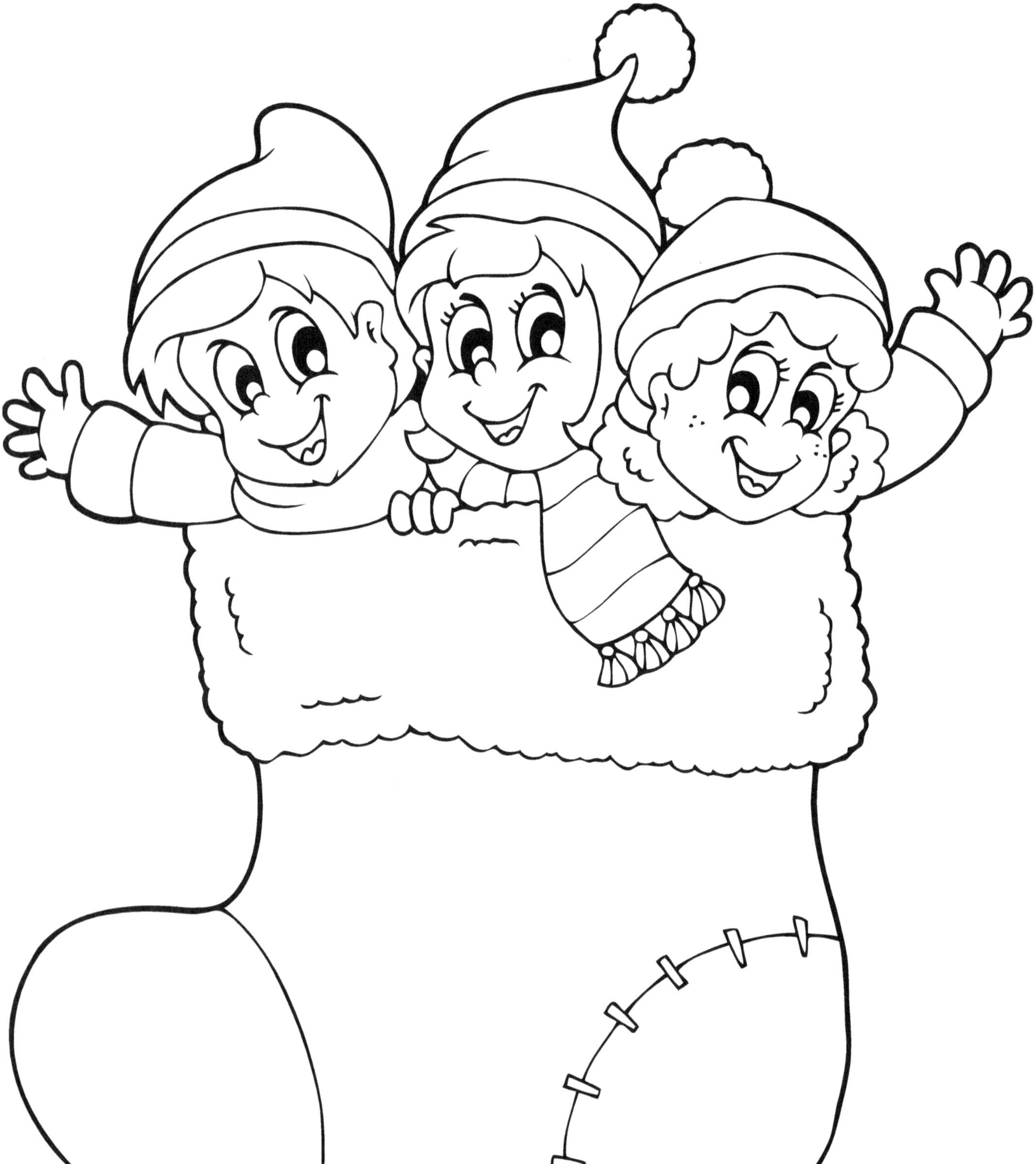

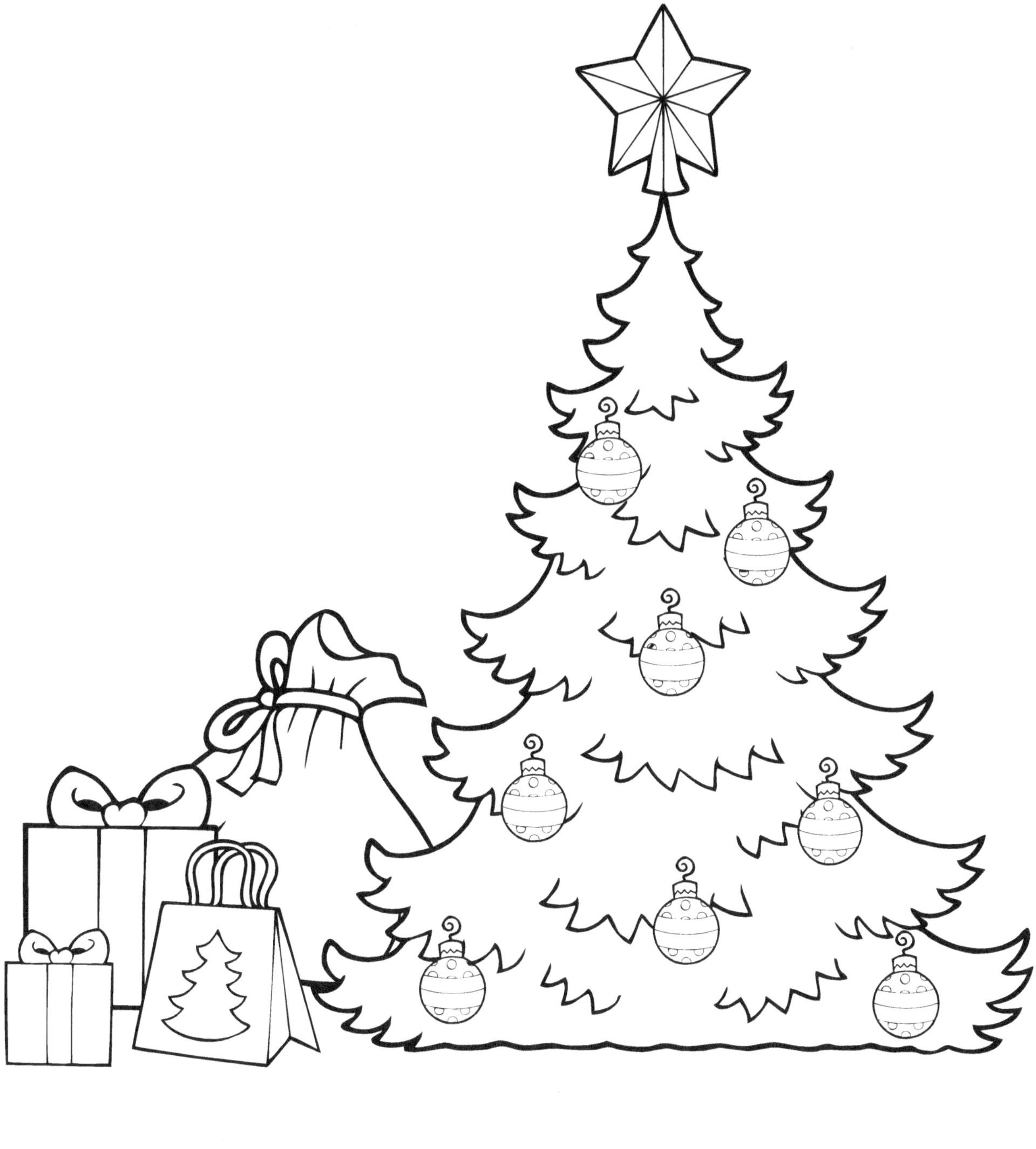

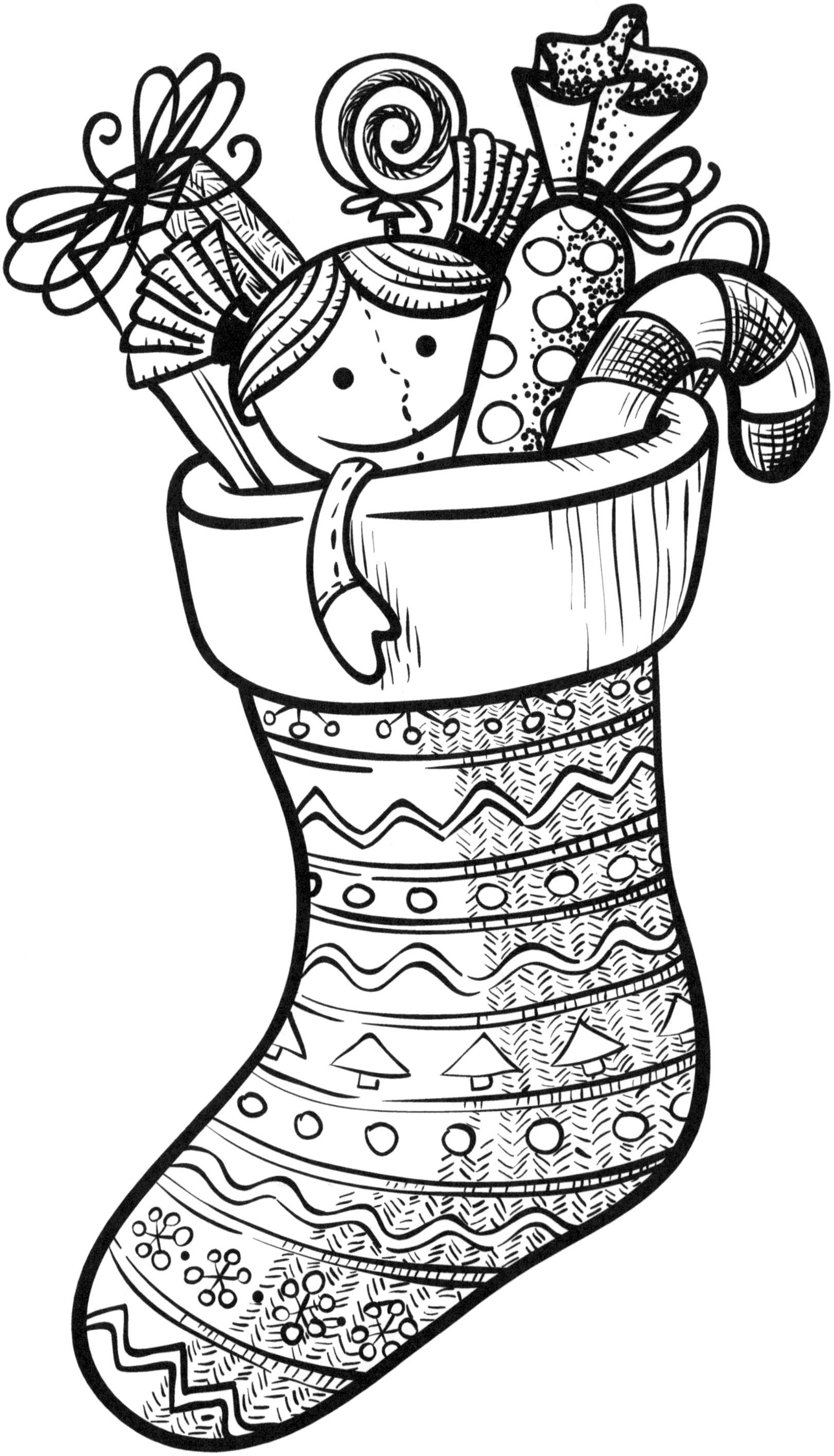

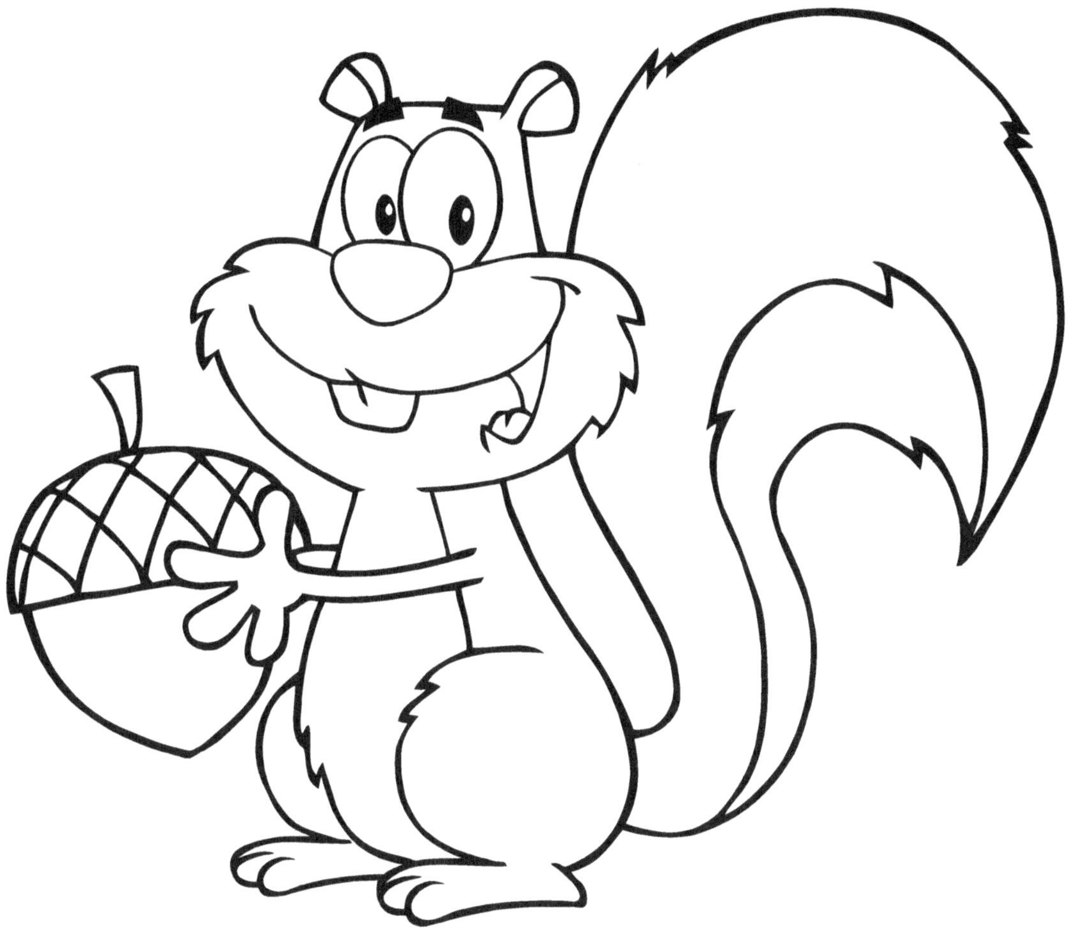

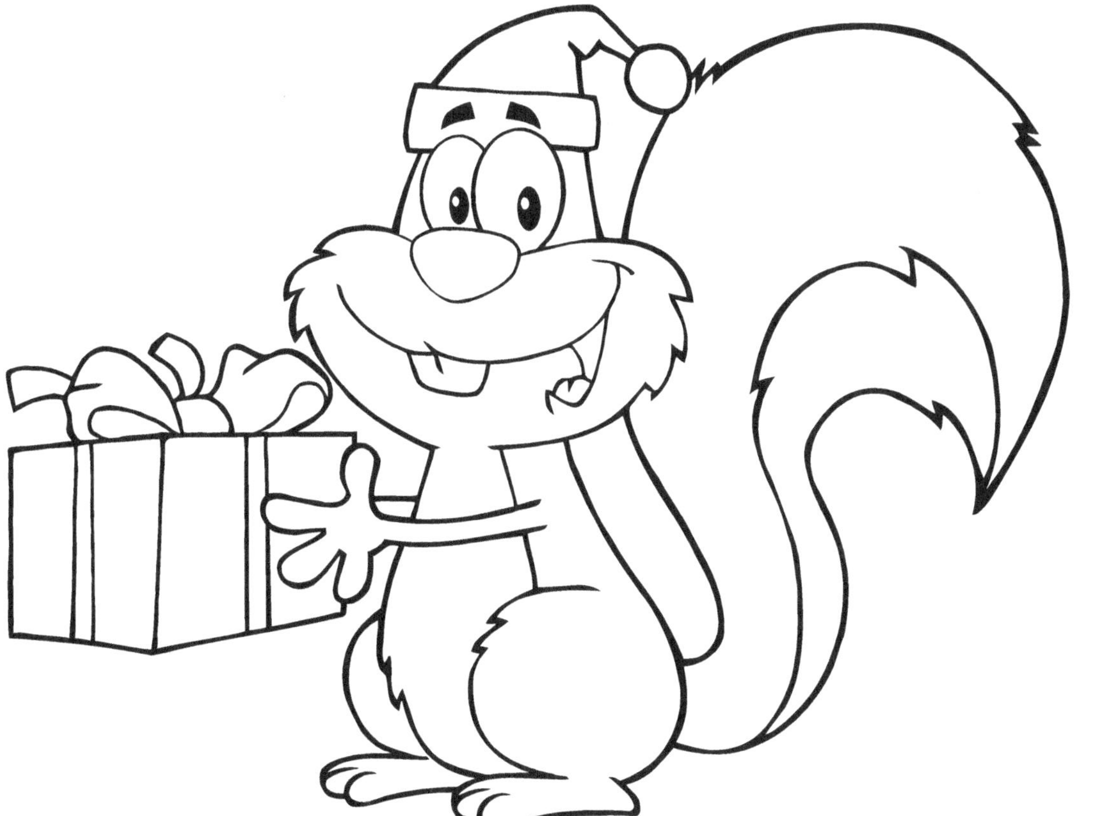

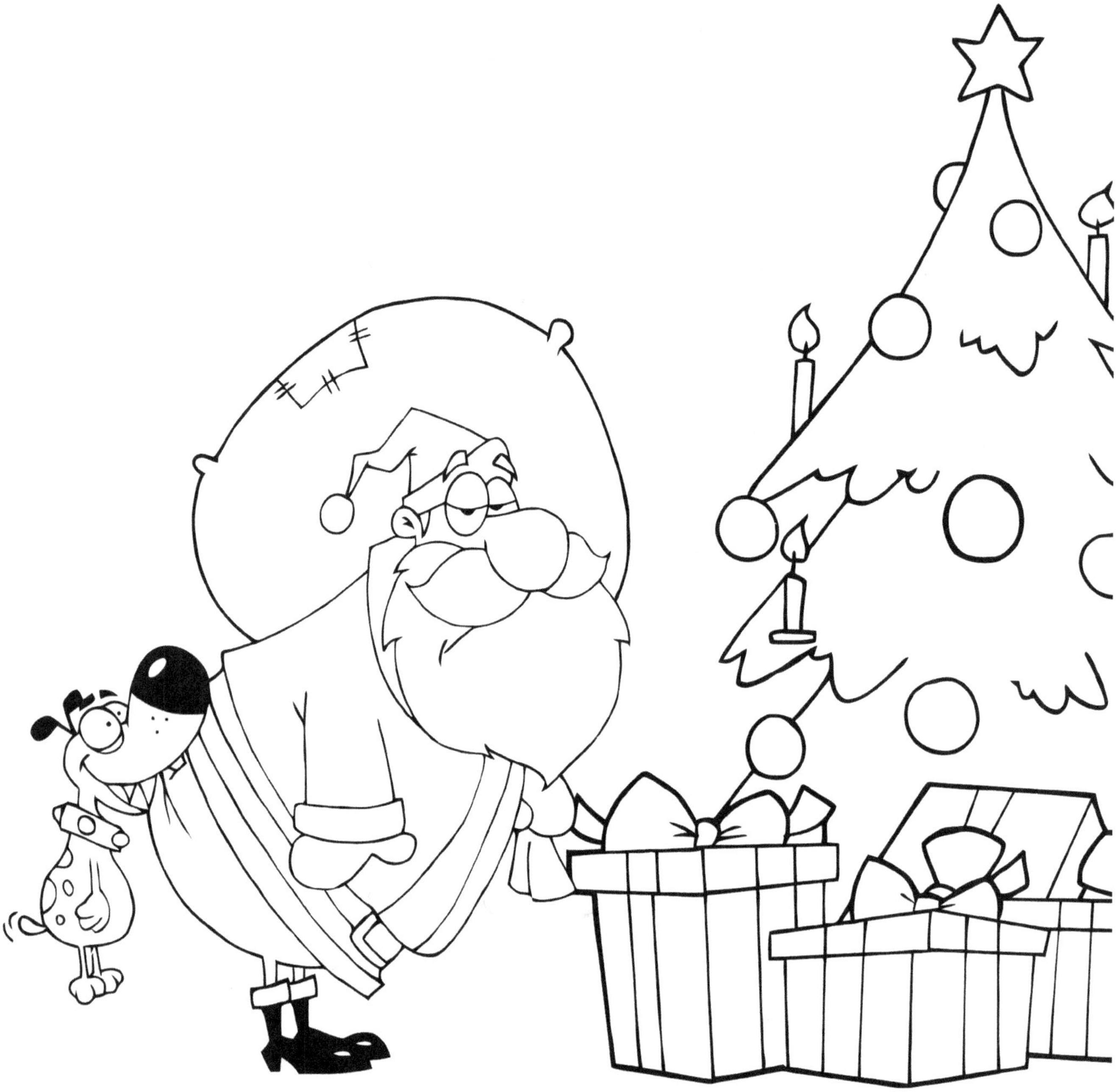

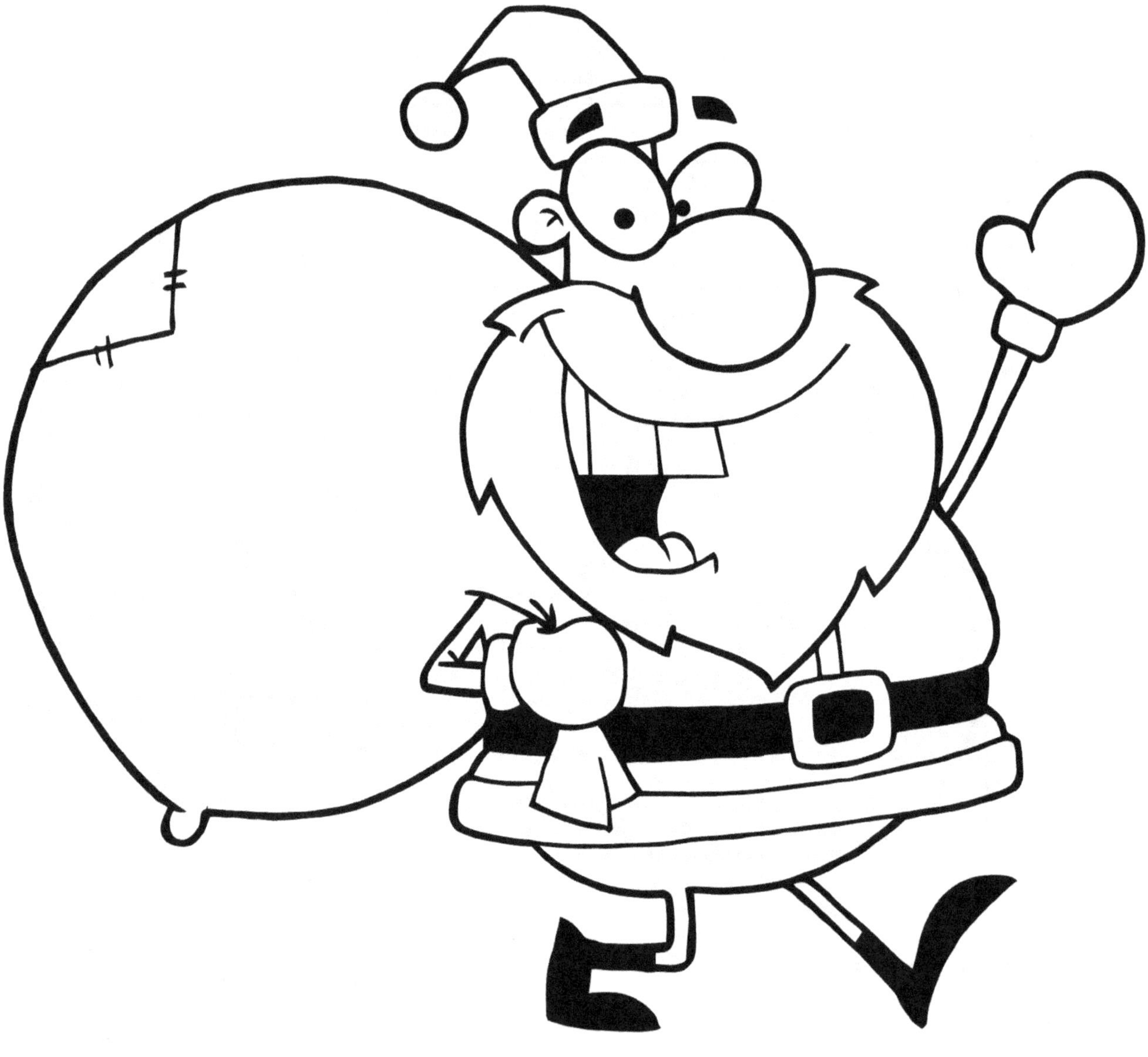

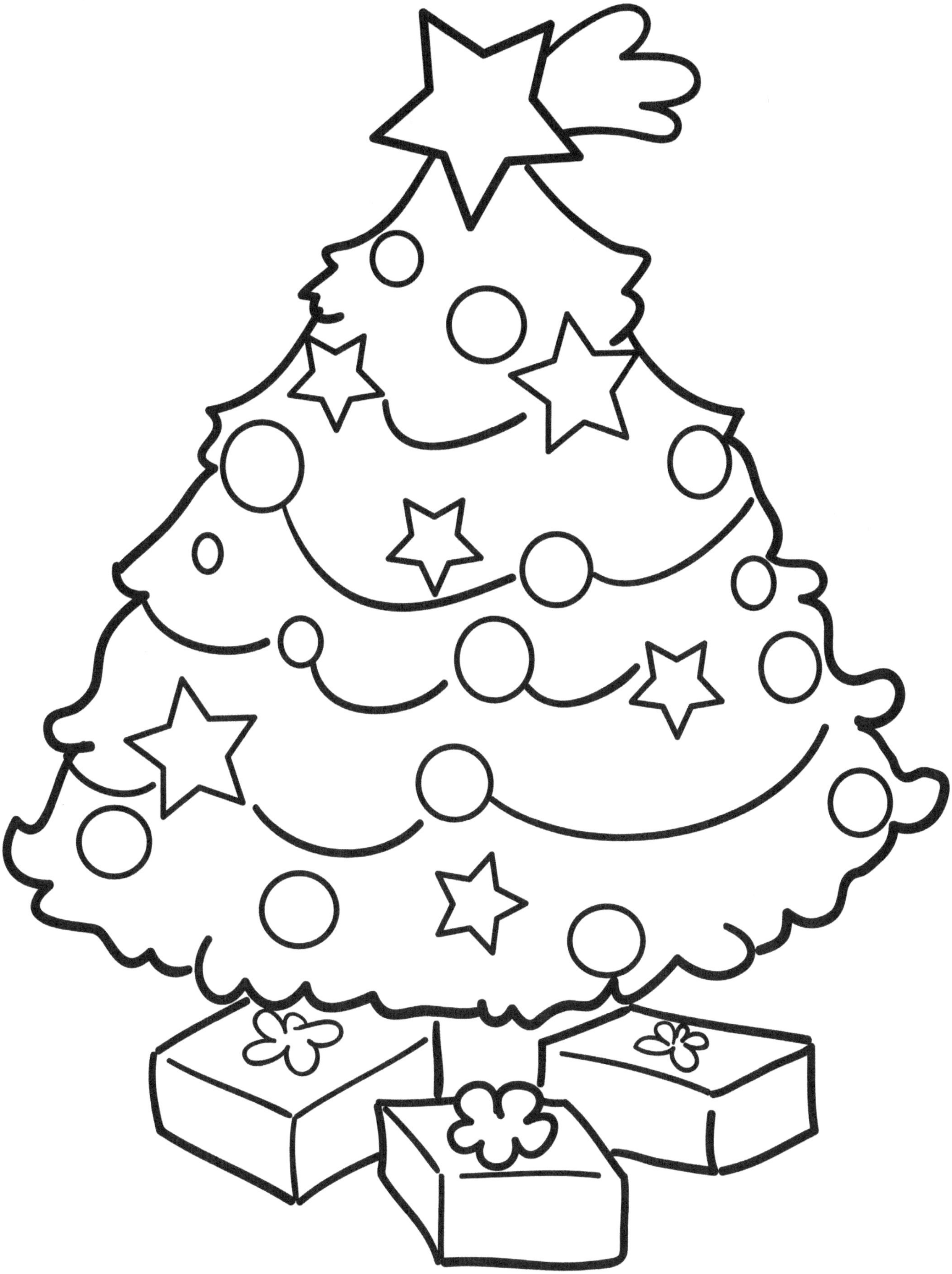

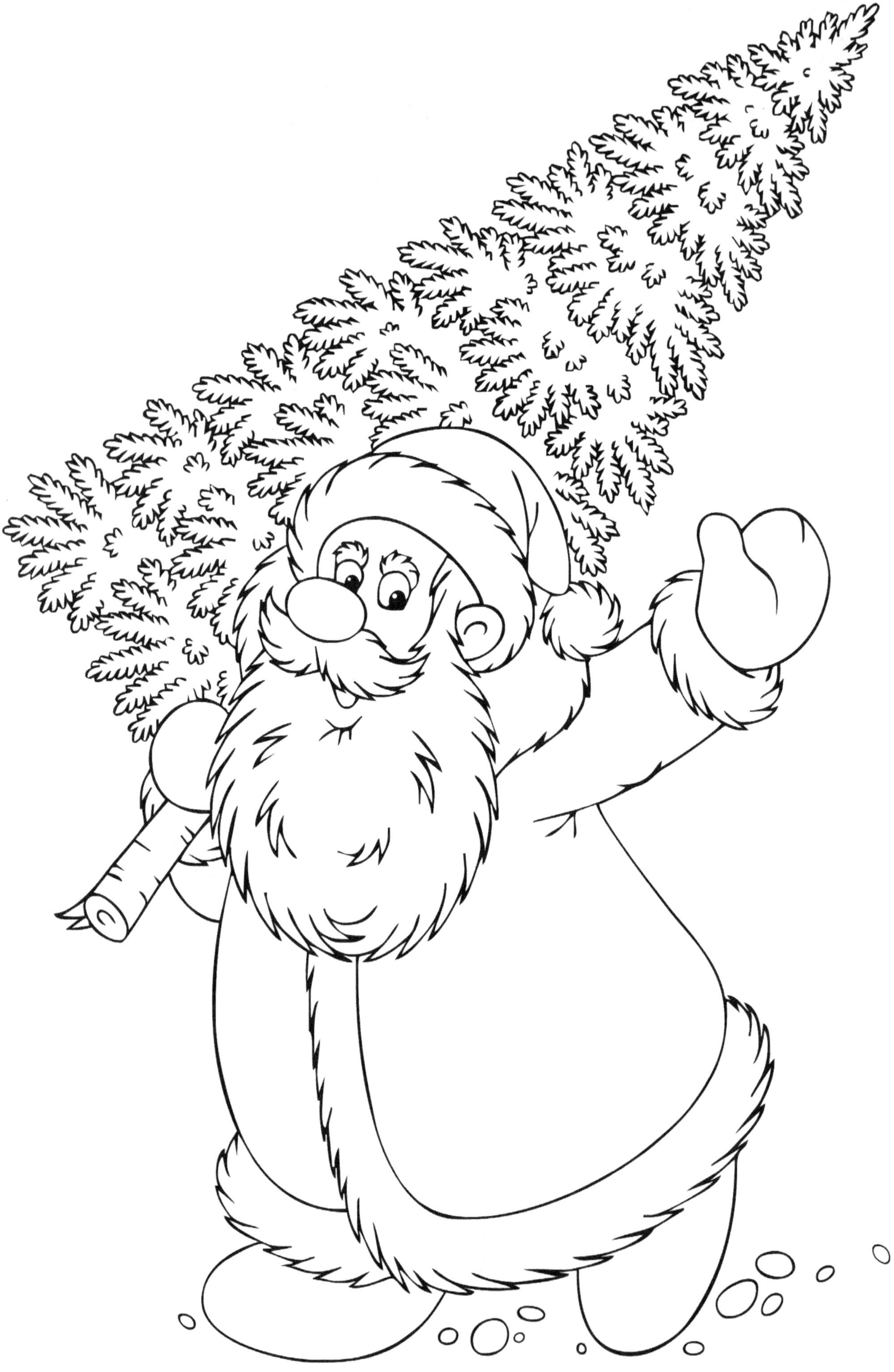

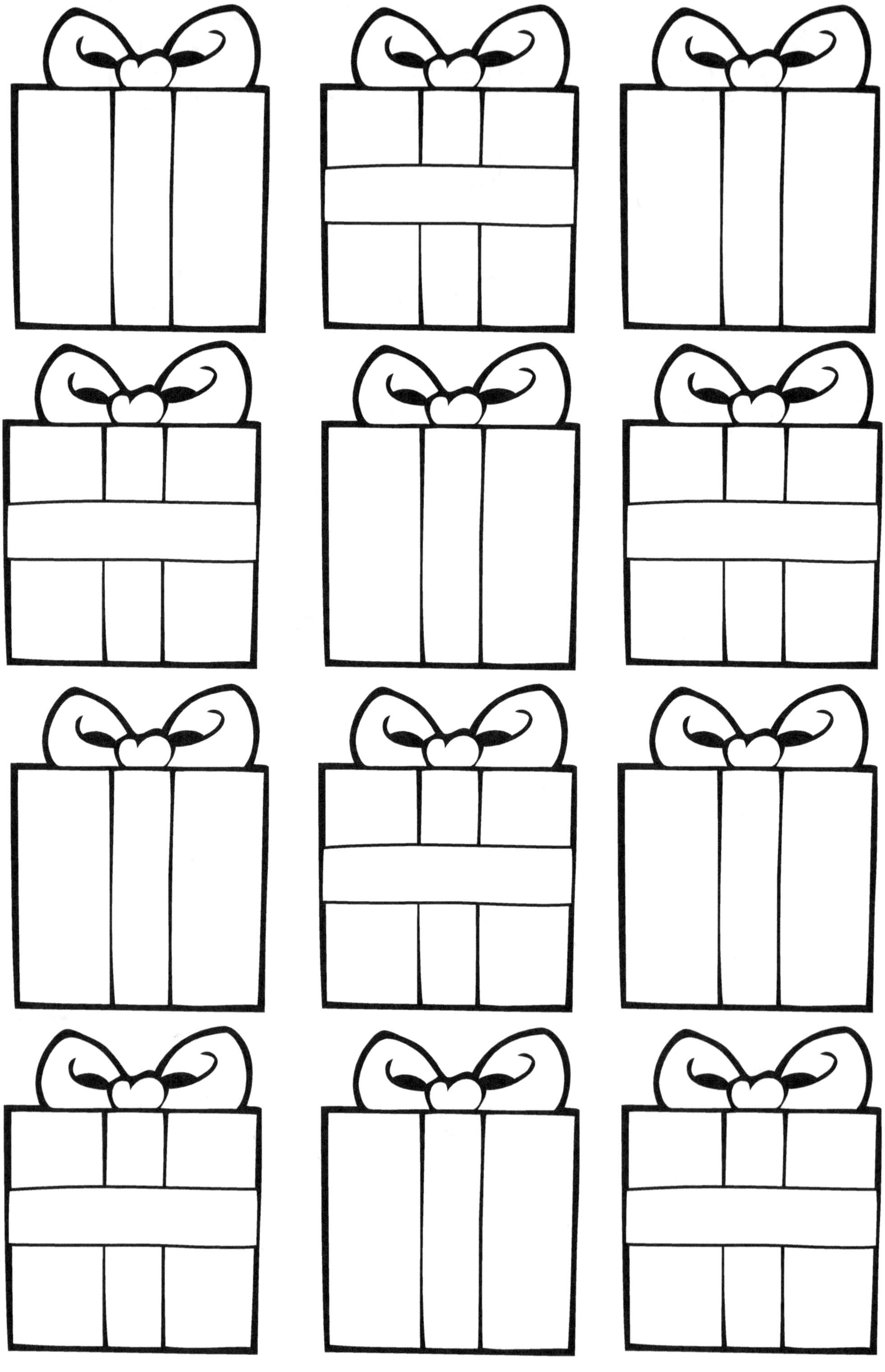

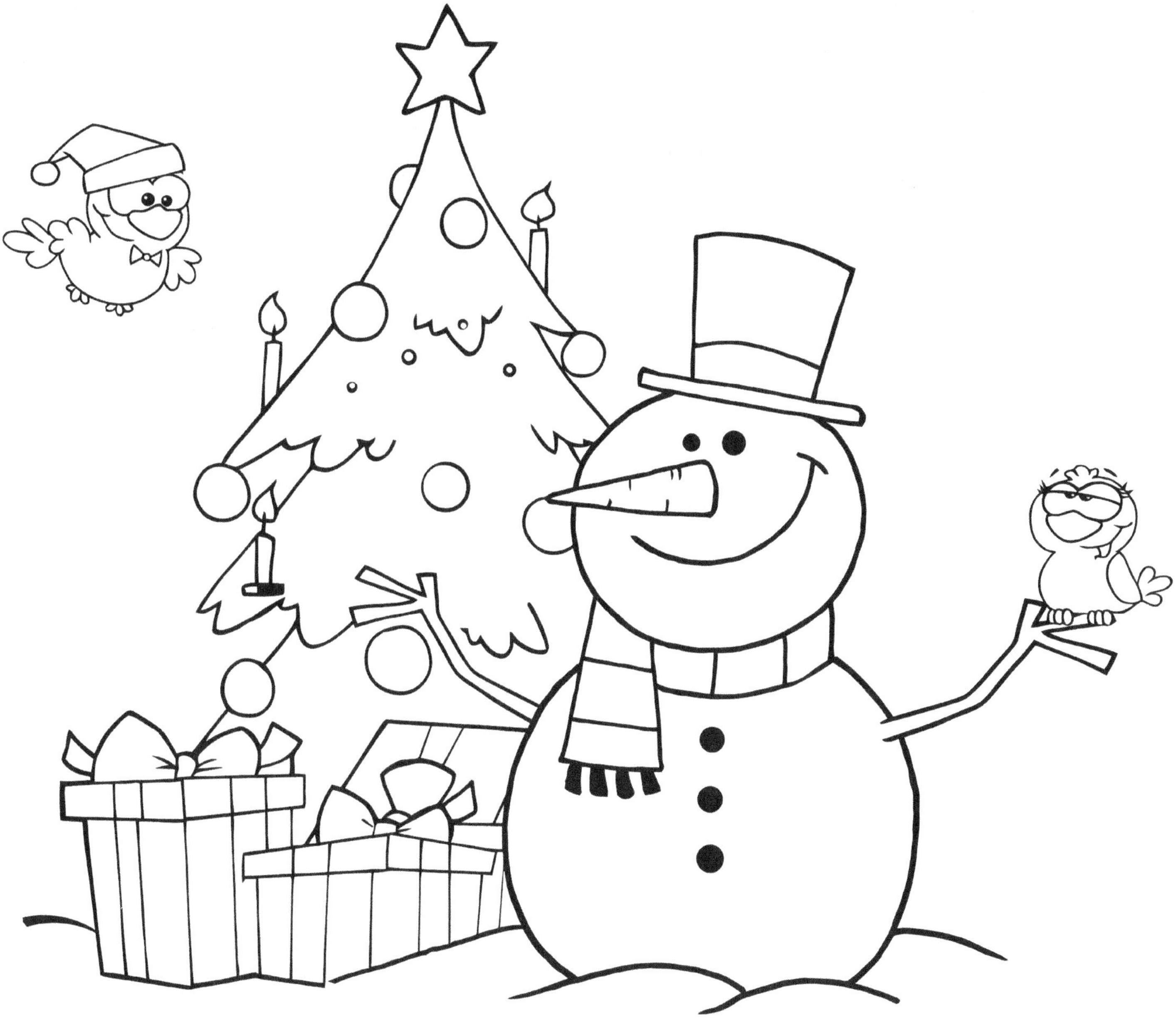

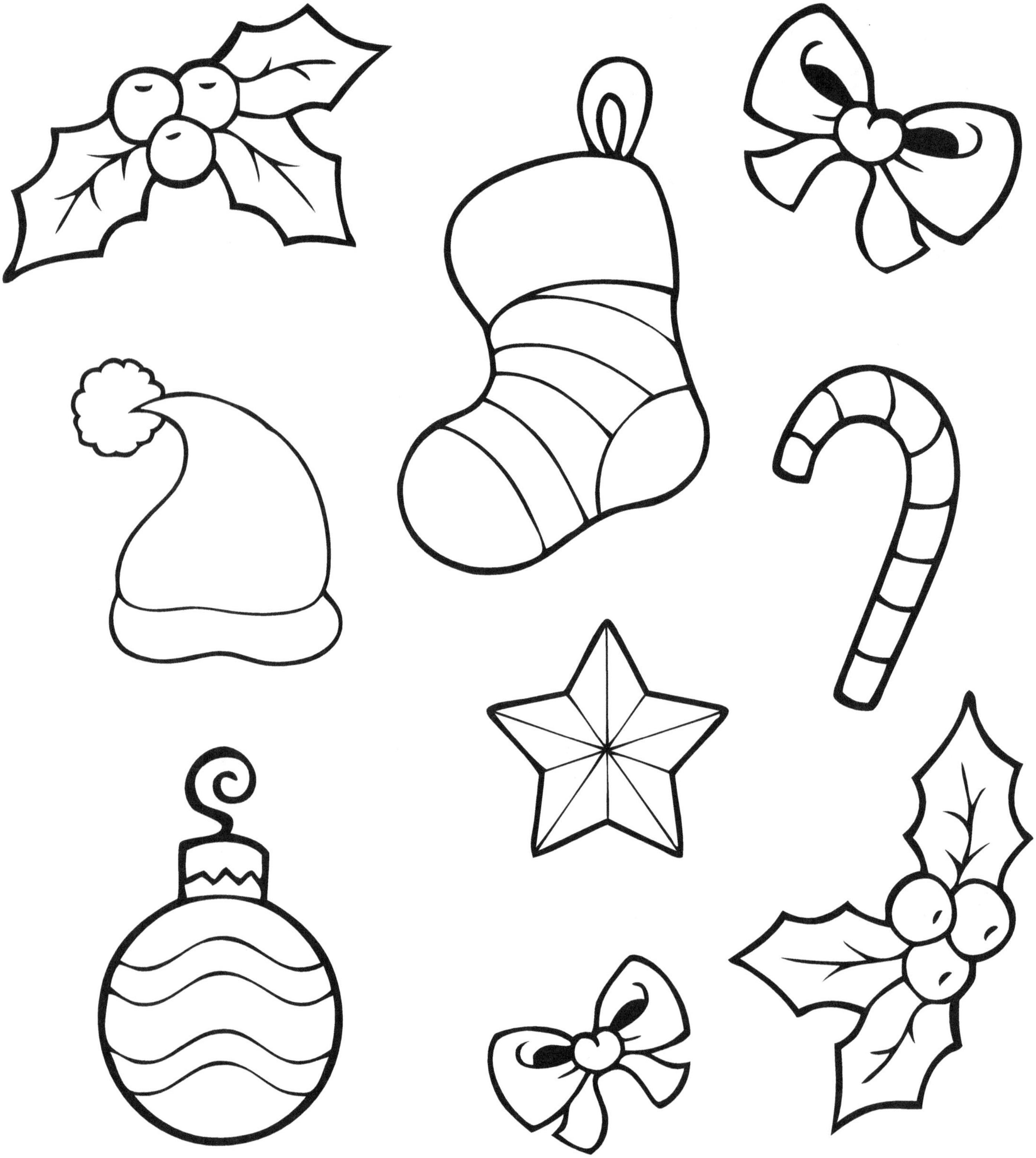

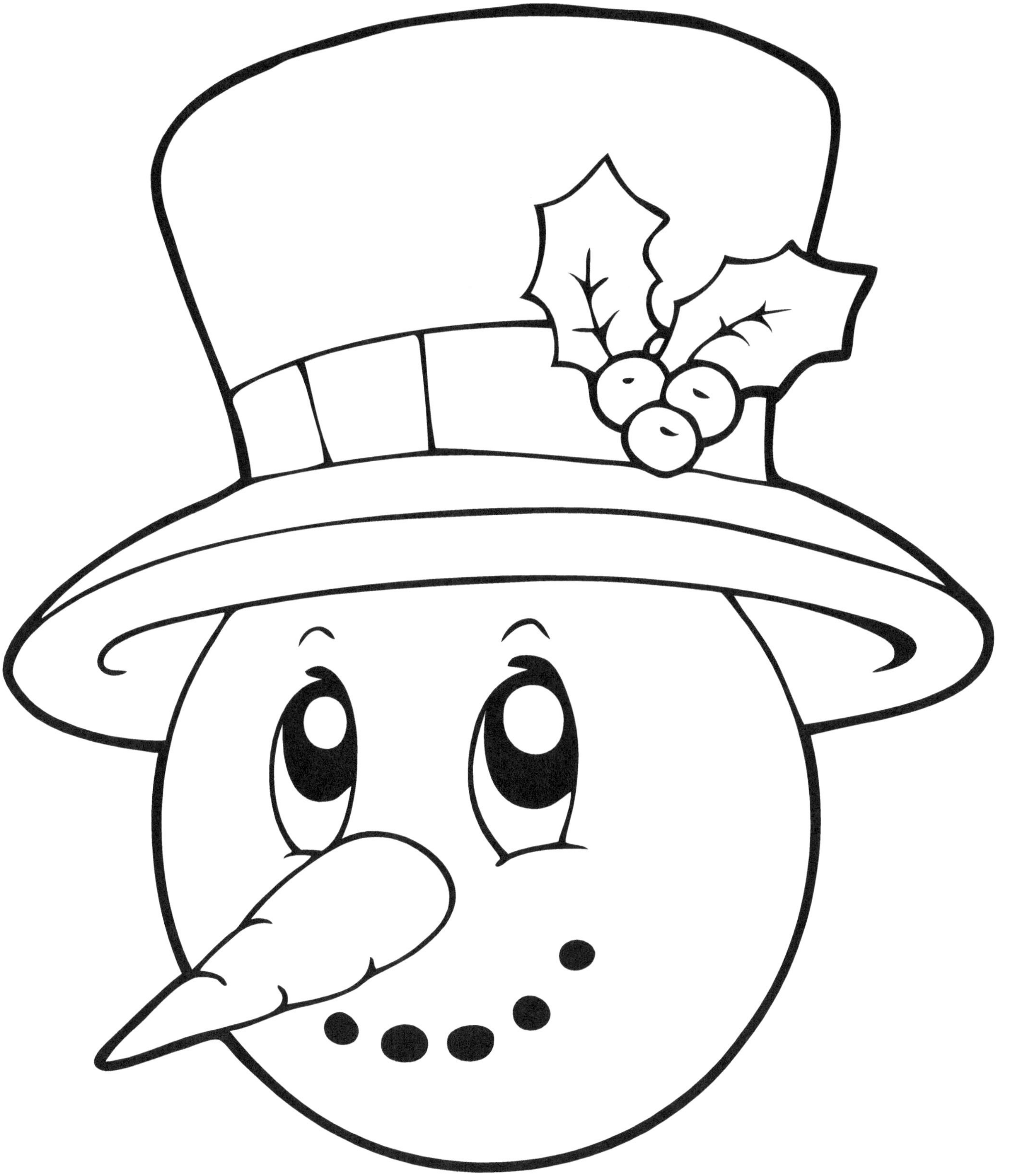

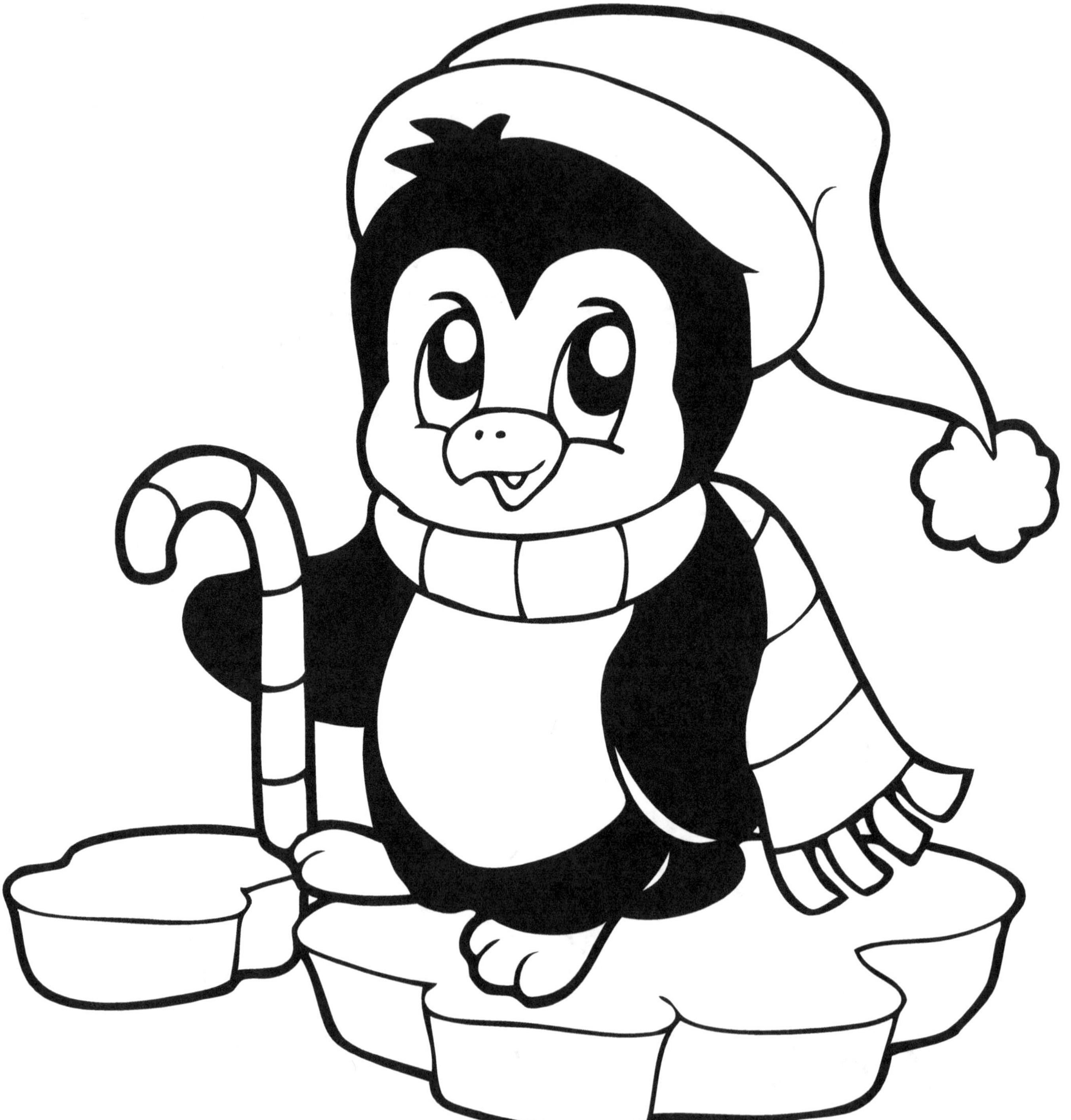

www.ingramcontent.com/pod-product-compliance
Lightning Source LLC
Chambersburg PA
CBHW062337220526
45469CB00008B/2753
9781785950766